LIFE, DEATH,
AND EVERYTHING IN-BETWEEN

By

Gloria Daniels

LIFE, DEATH,
AND EVERYTHING IN-BETWEEN

By

Gloria Daniels

Bladensburg, MD

LIFE, DEATH, AND EVERYTHING IN-BETWEEN

Published by
Inscript Books
a division of Dove Christian Publishers
P.O. Box 611
Bladensburg, MD 20710-0611
www.dovechristianpublishers.com

Copyright © 2020 by Gloria Daniels

Cover Design by Nadia Chatsworth

ISBN: 978-1-7348625-4-6

All rights reserved. No part of this publication may be used or reproduced without permission of the publisher, except for brief quotes for scholarly use, reviews or articles.

Published in the United States of America
25 24 23 22 21 20   1 2 3 4 5

Dedication

For my five wonderful daughters: Briana, Jessica, Angel, Alleah, and Alexis and nine adorable grandchildren. You all are the wind beneath my wings! Most of all, I dedicate this to the memory of my late son, Paul Brian Trammell, II, whose untimely death taught me the lessons about life, death, and everything in-between.

Contents

Preface	ix
Introduction	xvii
The Spirit Speaks, Moves, and Reveals.	1
Beware of Angels	13
Put Away the Impure Princes of False Religion	21
Messages from Heaven	27
If There's a Heaven, There Must Be a Hell	33
Satan, That Serpent of Ole and The Host of Fallen Angels	57
It's Time to Get Honest	65
There's a Time for Everything Under the Sun	83
If You Eat of the Tree, You Shall Truly Die	95
Where Do We Go from Here?	105
Sheol, The First Resting Place	109
His Sickness Won't End in Death	145
The Grand Final Destination of Heaven	167
The Fingerprints of Transition	181
Angelic Visitation	195
A Cloud by Day and a Fire by Night	203
Heavenly Gifts	207
The End of the Matter	227

Preface

There's a large, rainbow-colored elephant in the room and we do not want to acknowledge its presence. However, choosing to ignore it will not make it go away. This defiant creature will be there at some point directly and indirectly in every individual's life. Nonetheless, until we face it eye-to-eye, then we will never truly be free to live our lives in freedom or in full measure.

Perhaps you are entertaining a bit of suspense at this point. So, allow me to introduce you to this rainbow-pigmented entity. I would like for you to meet Death! Immediately, we envision in our mind's eye a black figure that lurks its dark silhouette in the shadows of life's light, a creature right out of Hollywood's theatrics. However, the slithering passiveness of this depiction is not as threatening until it's sitting right in the middle of the room of life, staring at us while clinching a loved one's hand at their bedside or ushering in the gripping, troublesome, sudden, or tragic death of a loved one. That passive depiction now becomes vehemently aggressive with large sharp fangs in a huge salivating mouth and piercing claws that has taken on the form of a creature right out of a Steven Spielberg horror movie. With this horrific picture in our minds-eye, we shudder at the remote thought of Death for ourselves or that precious loved one.

But what if God desires to turn this configuration about this inevitable and most natural part of life and shift it from the rainbow-colored elephant in the room that is too difficult to confront to embracing the rainbow of His promise of being the "Resurrection and the Life?" Do we really understand the knowledge that He was trying to dispatch to our souls? If not, take a deep breath and exhale slowly as you brace yourself for an impactful time of rediscovering life. For if we can understand death, then we can understand everything there is about life. Therefore, we can embrace everything else in-between with confidence and optimism that we have a hope and a future, regardless of what our unpredictable probationary period of time on earth entails, especially during times that produce emotional, mental, or physical scars.

This life is simply a dress rehearsal and not the final curtain call or grand finale in God's playbill for His creation. I hope that by the end of this book, you will have learned that Life, Death, and Everything In-Between are a divine spiritual continuum that's co-mingled together, like beautiful pieces of a mosaic that are connected together to form a magnificent work of art. Although the earth is governed by time and space, Heaven has no such confinements. However, we see clearly with the use of the word "as," a conjunction that denotes that something is happening while something else is taking place, that Heaven and earth are linear coordinates on the continuum with life, death, and everything in-between.

A significant loss of mine serves as the backdrop of this story. However, the Holy Spirit shone a beacon of light from the lighthouse of God's heart that found me right in the midst of the storm of tragedy. In due time, God handcrafted the true purpose of my life before I was ever placed in my mother's womb. Nothing catches Him by surprise. He knew that I would have a son and have to bury that son. Albeit, He already knew the vastness of the gift that He had orchestrated for me to enrich this spiritual discourse about life and death. He doesn't just pitch something to us "off the cuff" in a catch-and-release fashion. Yet, often the hard taskmaster of our humanity may perceive His mode of operation in our lives as contrite, careless, and frivolous when we cannot fully trace His hand. But ***Jeremiah 29:11*** navigates the hand and heart of God for us: **"For I know the plans that I have in mind for you," declares Adonai, "plans for shalom and not calamity—to give you a future and a hope"**.

Shalom is the Hebrew word for "peace." It is this hope that serves as the driving force to trust Him in ALL things. He is not a mortal, double-minded man that can lie, nor is He a son of mere unpredictable men that changes His mind ***(Numbers 23:19)***. However, we all have experienced times of what felt like pure calamity in our lives and certainly knew that He couldn't truly be a good God and love us if we are suffering through this agony in our broken matrix called life. No matter what calamity falls upon our lives, God's plans for us are always for peace, a future, and a hope. This doesn't change. It is and will always be His desire for His beloved creation made in His very own image. However, we can make choices as freewill beings that are contrary to God's planned purpose. So, therefore, we may become our own culprits of situations that rob us of a future, hope, and peace.

But living in a fallen world with an adversary that's strongly against God and His creation, we are enlisted into a spiritual battle that separates life, which, in turn, produces death. Nonetheless, take heart that God has left us with the GPS to navigate every gradient of the uphill climb of this life to our final destination. The aspects of "life after life," a phrase coined by Raymond Moody, a pioneer and researcher of near-death experiences, must be prepared for with just as much fervor as this temporary life, if not more. A patient once said to me, "Living is hard. Death is easy." Perhaps this was King Solomon's understanding as he states these words: *"I applied my heart to seek and examine by wisdom all that is done under heaven What a burdensome task God has given the sons of men to keep them occupied. I have seen all the deeds done under the sun; and behold, all is meaningless and chasing after the wind" Ecclesiastes 1:13-14.*

These sobering words were written by the wisest and wealthiest man that had ever existed. If you ever read the whole book of Ecclesiastes, it can propel you into the throes of despair about life. Solomon was merely conveying the same concept of earthly living that I'm guiding us through today. This life and all that we achieve and obtain is ONLY TEMPORARY, and we don't get to take any of it with us into life after life! So if ALL that matters to you is "living your best life," as we express in our modern vernacular, then you have completely missed the point of your existence on this earth and your existence to come after your life no longer abides on this earth.

A familiar phrase by the theologian Lynn H. Hough, *"Life is a journey, not a destination,"* is the very essence of living this momentary life that is like a vapor. ***James 4:14*** clearly illustrates this poignant fact: *"Yet you do not know what your life will be like tomorrow. What is your life? For you are a vapor that appears for a little while and then vanishes".* In the grand scheme of eternity, our life is only a day. Therefore, Simon Peter portrays it this way in ***2 Peter 3:8***: *"But don't forget this one thing, loved ones, that with the Lord one day is like a thousand years, and a thousand years are like one day."* Furthermore, King David conveys in ***Psalm 90:4***, *"For a thousand years in your sight are like a day just passing by or like a watch in the night."* During my recent study of the Apocrypha Books of the Bible, I read in the following ***Book of Jubilees 4:29-30***: *"And at the close of the nineteenth jubilee, in the seventh week in the sixth year [930 A.M.] thereof, Adam died, and all his sons buried him in the land of his creation, and he was the first to be buried in the earth. And he lacked seventy years of one thousand years; for one thousand years are as one day in the testimony of the heavens and therefore was it written concerning the tree of knowledge: 'On the day that ye eat thereof ye shall die.' For this reason, he did not complete the years of this day; for he died during it."* We know that Adam died at age 930, and in a logical earthly context, that was an enormous amount of many, many days. However, in the heavenly exchange system, it takes 1000 years to equal one day. Therefore, in the mind of God, Adam did not live one day! Conversely, if we can grasp this profound realization, figuratively speaking, our one day with the Lord will be greater than a lifetime on earth!

It is our final destination that will remain for all eternity, and our efforts and consciousness must heed to this truth. In as much, all cultures and ethnicities are trained and educated to prepare with all of our might for this temporary existence of earthly living. We strive to prosper by obtaining financial and familial success, as this is believed to provide "a good life." We put such fervent intentional and purposeful focus into preparing for a vacation, job interviews, business opportunities, a wedding, starting a family, buying a house, a new car, or a career—all the temporary aspects of life that can't and won't last forever. However, we do very little to prepare for everlasting eternal life, which every living individual will face.

John presented a scriptural basis for hoping that the members of the Church would prosper and be healthy. Nonetheless, there's an additional component that often gets pushed aside, which is our soul and spiritual life prospering. John admonished them with these words in 3 John 2:

"Dear friend, I am praying that everything prosper with you and that you be in good health, as I know you are prospering spiritually" (CJB).

"Loved ones, I pray that all may go well with you and that you may be in good health, just as it is well with your soul". This perhaps is the basis for much of our modern "prosperity gospel" of health and wealth.

Therefore, we must not neglect this vital segment of our soul flourishing with the divine interconnectedness with the Source of all living things. The Messiah exhorted us to not let this fleeting world be more important than our souls. *"For what does it profit a man to gain the whole world, yet forfeit his soul? For what could a man give in exchange for his soul?" Mark 8:36.* This is a rhetorical question. Furthermore, *"Do not store up for yourselves treasures on earth, where moth and rust destroy and where thieves break in and steal. But store up for yourselves treasures in heaven, where neither moth nor rust destroys and where thieves do not break in or steal. For where your treasure is, there will your heart be also" Matthew 6:18-21.*

You can live in the grandest home and drive the finest top of the line automobile but then be completely impoverished in your very soul that will continue to live on with your immortal spirit when you draw your last breath. Therefore, beloved, let's allow our soul to prosper with the spiritual awareness of His miraculous reverent wonders that are beyond this natural earth and embrace the supernatural realms crafted by the Master Builder. Let's allow ourselves to be transformed and to prosper spiritually; better yet, let's go a step further by seeking the deep and hidden things of

God. Can we embrace life's unique spiritual mysteries and their concessions with this earthly dimension?

The Bible is just as equally impactful about death as it is life. In contrast, it's easy to skirt these passages because they are not the particular ones that give us goosebumps from excitement. Nonetheless, God's word has purpose and meaning to guide us into all truth about Life, Death, and Everything In-between. Being a student of the afterlife could be viewed as morbid and unhealthy or perhaps bear the resemblance of a dark personality. Nonetheless, let's take a deep dive into shifting this philosophical school of thought about the afterlife and institute the divine counsel of the Lord that He equipped us with. I realized that when I started writing, I was a student about life and death. After countless hours of researching the scriptures, near-death experiences, and the incredible downloads from the Holy Spirit, now the student has become the teacher. So, let's begin the lessons about Life, Death, and Everything In-between.

Introduction

We want to avoid suffering, death, sin, ashes. But we live in a world crushed and broken and torn, a world God Himself visited to redeem. We receive his poured-out life, and being allowed the high privilege of suffering with Him, may then pour ourselves out for others." ~ Elisabeth Elliot

Welcome to an audacious journey that will launch you into the deep waters of your faith or challenge the lack thereof. We will walk down a vicarious path into magnificent spiritual experiences that are beyond the natural confinements of this earth. The Lord has produced exceedingly and abundantly more than I could have ever imagined by teaching me profound Rhema revelations from His word about Life, Death, and Everything In-between.

Most books about death are about working through grief or the death and dying process from a hospice or palliative care perspective. Nonetheless, this is not going to be that kind of self-help focus on how to cope with grief or what to expect during the stages of impending death in terminal illness. Having previous experience as a hospice nurse, I have a deep appreciation for this genre of education. Nonetheless, there are significant spiritual impartations contained in these pages that may assuredly help anyone who may be grieving, no matter if the loss occurred one year ago or twenty.

Within this book lies one of the most honest scrutinies about death and life, from a definitive spiritual concept, that you may have ever read. The intention is to bring truth to our schools of thought, misinformation, and misconceptions about what brought death to earth's domain and who is ultimately responsible for it. The mission is to shift our mindset from how we commonly view death into how we can embrace death from a true biblical perspective. This will break the yoke that holds us in bondage to its fear and its pain. We strive to understand the strata about life, but we are very apprehensive to do the same about death. It takes faith and courage beyond ourselves to seek answers to the greatest conundrum of life, what happens when we die, and its incorporation with the unseen realms of the afterlife.

Death and grief are two very unwelcomed parts of our lives, and I definitely didn't envision it becoming a part of mine in the manner in which it did. However, this was precisely the overzealous commodity of pain that stripped my soul bare, with the sudden loss of my 27-year-old precious son on May 29, 2016. I'm astonished how the Father knew what tapestry that He had intricately knitted together by His heavenly design to cover and console my utter despair. Through the evolution of this book, He exchanged my ash heap for beauty to reveal His love and glory, even in the midst of the agony. He foretold that this was precisely one of the reasons that He came, as the Prophet Isaiah describes in **_Isaiah 61:2-3, "to comfort all who mourn, to console those who mourn in Zion, to give them beauty for ashes, the oil of joy for mourning, the garment of praise for the spirit of heaviness, that they might be called oaks of righteousness, the planting of Adonai, that He may be glorified."_**

God's hope for His children is to fulfill our own unique individual purposes and plans that He outlined for us before the foundations of the world were laid. I would have never predicted that my purpose would be derived from the most painfully

Introduction

agonizing experience of my existence. I have said numerous times throughout the years that one day I would become an author. I have chosen nursing as a profession, and although I am very passionate about my career calling, I knew that was not my purpose. I intuitively knew that there was a significant story waiting to be written inside me. Through the years, I would put pen to paper or fingers to keyboard, only to instinctively know that this was not it; this was not the story, and this was not the time. The Lord tells us to not lean on what we can understand or make sense of. But in everything we do, acknowledge Him, and He will direct our journey *(Proverbs 3:5-6)*. But I always knew that whenever and whatever would birth the story, it would be a non-fiction literary work. I make this point to direct your attention to the fact that all of the supernatural experiences that I will share are not fictional. This is not a fictitious story or a fairy tale, although mere human logic may cause you to entertain that suggestion. Be that as it may, as I begin to unfold my supernatural encounters, you may think that you are reading the script of a science fiction movie or novel. Perhaps it would make a good one, except it really happened to me. I can replay these experiences so vividly that it's like watching reruns of a favorite show.

At some point, we will all be curious about what happens when we die. The scientific-minded may believe in the theory of oblivion, which is the state of complete non-existence after death. So, in other words, lights out forever and ever. Every culture and religion has beliefs about the afterlife and those places that exist in another world beyond this one, such as Heaven and Hell or other forms of similar underworlds. Many philosophers such as Plato and Socrates, along with Greek mythical legends, have vibrant and colorful accounts of what happens in the hereafter.

DISCLAIMER: This book bears no belief or adherence to New Age religion, mysticism, channeling, mediumship, or psychic practices or beliefs. Perhaps you have believed more so in New Age concepts and intellectual diadems that tell you that the universe is a force that is guiding the steps of your life, or how to channel energy to reach higher levels of self. If that is the case, my heart yearns for you to have your heart and mind enlightened to the One and Only King of the Universe, Jesus Christ. I must expound on this segment because ***"I am in no mood to be deceived any longer by the crafty devil and false character whose greatest pleasure is to take advantage of everyone" ~ Camille Claudel***

Later, I will share a riveting true account about the Devil's use and perversion of the supernatural to a group of well-meaning Christians in a Bible study group that wanted to see angels. Seeking to see angels, deceased loved ones, or knowing the future can lead to blurred lines and produce schemes and deceptions of Satan and demonic entities. This can cause someone to believe the experiences are from God, but they are truly a counterfeit of the true craftsmanship of God's created heavenly realms and angelic beings. Before I reveal my experience of the large heavenly being that was sent as a warning that something was looming in the atmosphere the day before my son died, I want us to understand critical principles about dealing with supernatural experiences.

Supernatural encounters occur in a variety of ways, such as dreams, visions, and direct manifestations of spiritual entities. Consequently, there are two very real facets to the supernatural: One being of God and angels and the other being of Satan and demons. There must be immense caution when dealing with the supernatural. Everything that looks good and sounds good is NOT good and most definitely is NOT God. Every encounter must be

Introduction

measured with the sound word of the Gospel. If it violates His word and character, then it is not of Him. It is inconsequential how good that it may make you "feel" or what you believe that you heard or saw. Many cults and false religions have been formed because of the tickling of the ears from false teachings, doctrines, and demonic events. We will examine the importance of understanding these principles that God left us with in dealing with the supernatural or paranormal if you will, in one of our lessons. Let's recall that the student has become the teacher about life, death, and everything in-between.

I will share the incredible gift from my Heavenly Father, of an open vision of being able to see my son's transition from this life into the afterlife. The afterlife is REAL! PARADISE IS REAL! Angelic Beings are not little fat babies with wings and halos floating on clouds and playing harps. These miraculous events began when He allowed me to see the ten-foot-tall angelic being, with a flame emanating from its opaque form, in the still of the night at 3 o'clock in the morning in my backyard, the day before my son crossed over. I will take you on an obstacle course of climatic events that started with this event. Additionally, although this was beyond a wonderful experience, this pales in comparison to the encounter that was waiting for me at the cusp of all things that are Holy, Just, and True. So, brace yourselves as I share the in-depth, full details about these marvelous experiences.

To enumerate through these experiences and the revelation that the Holy Spirit has endowed me with, the world's view and ideas about life and death have been completely transformed by the renewing of my mind to the word of God. ***"Do not be conformed to this world but be transformed by the renewing of your mind, so that you may discern what is the will of God—what is good*** *and acceptable and perfect" Romans 12:2.* He desires for us to be renewed in our minds in all matters involving life, but even more so, death because they work together hand and hand. We cannot have one without the other. Therefore, I implore your undivided attention as I prepare a methodology for the renewing of your mind to the intricacies of life, death, and everything in-between. We are going to boldly face the elephant in the room.

Contained throughout this manuscript are sound biblical supplications grounded in the word of God. I once heard that the acronym for the BIBLE is "Basic instructions before leaving earth." That sums it up perfectly. The word of God declares: ***"All Scripture is inspired by God and useful for teaching, for reproof, for restoration, and for training in righteousness, so that the person belonging to God may be capable, fully equipped for every good deed" 2 Timothy 3:17.***

"The grass withers, the flower fades but the word of our God will stand forever" Isaiah 40:8 (ESV).

"And we also thank God continually because, when you received the word of God, which you heard from us, you accepted it not as a human word, but as it actually is, the word of God, which is indeed at work in you who believe" 1 Thessalonians 2:13 (NIV).

Upon the initial glance of flipping through the pages, you may be unable to define exactly the genre of this book. Our human intellect has the need to construct a box and affix an appropriate label to make sense of things that we may not fully understand, particularly with spirituality. However, these Rhema revelations of the mysteries of God cannot be placed into a box! His power and glory cannot be manipulated and compressed into mortal men's intellectual receptacles! The divine spiritual encounters of life, death, and everything in-between cannot be jostled to fit into a box of men's ideologies and spiritual conjectures, "like a box of chocolates, you never know what you're gonna get." *"'Heaven is my throne,' says Adonai, 'and the earth is my footstool. What kind of house could you build for me? What sort of place could you devise for my rest?'" Isaiah 66:1 (CJB).* Clearly, The Father was conveying that we cannot create or construct anything that could possibly contain Him, in both contextual relationships of an earthly or spiritual confinement.

We cannot contain omniscience, His ability to know everything. We cannot challenge omnipotence; He's almighty and supreme. We cannot duplicate omnipresence, His ability to be everywhere at one time. He is the Hebrew word *niqqud*, which means, "I am who I am," "I will become what I choose to become," "I will be what I will be," or even, "I create whatever I create." Additionally, the most common English translation is "I am that I am." This is the summation of the nature of Elohim, YHWH, God.

Therefore, I must forego the attempt to classify this spiritual deluge of manifestations and instructions to share with the world. How can you enclose the God of the universe, who is so magnificent that His Spirit overshadowed a young virgin to place His Son, housed in flesh and blood as a baby, into her undefiled body and womb?

"O the depth of the riches, both of the wisdom and knowledge of God! How unsearchable are His judgments and how incomprehensible His ways. For 'who has known the mind of Adonai, or who has been His counselor?' Or 'who has first given to Him, that it shall be repaid to him?'" Romans 11:33-35.

I Corinthians 1:26-27 is the summation of what we may count as foolishness from the world's perspective and are the very things that God will choose to stupefy the world's ideas of strength, wisdom, and power.

"For you see your calling, brothers and sisters, that not many are wise according to human standards, not many are powerful, and not many are born well. Yet God chose the foolish things of the world so He might put to shame the wise; and God chose the weak things of the world so He might put to shame the strong."

Therefore, God's plan to send His Son to earth just to die so we could return to Him and have eternal life is completely foolish to man's intellect. On the contrary, we must depend on the Holy Spirit to help us understand the spiritual things that the limited human mind cannot comprehend. ***1 Corinthians 2:14 (NIV)*** declares, *"The person without the Spirit does not accept the things that come from the Spirit of God but considers them foolishness, and cannot understand them because they are discerned only through the Spirit."* Perhaps some or even all of this book may seem foolish to your intellect or even challenge your religious beliefs, because it most certainly did mine. But that's the goodness and beauty of God's workmanship in our lives that is fluid and building line upon line and precept upon precept just as Isaiah spoke of in Chapter 28:9-10: *"To whom will He teach knowledge? To whom will He explain the message? Those just weaned from milk? Those just taken from the breast? For it must be precept upon precept, percept upon precept, line upon line, line upon line, here a little, there a little."*

Jesus is the Savior and Lord of my life; therefore, allow me to introduce you to my trusted and faithful co-author and Helper, The Holy Spirit. My favorite analogy, when describing the Spirit of God, is the wind. ***John 3:8*** states that *"the wind blows where it wishes, and you hear its sound, but you do not know where it*

Introduction

comes from or where it goes. So it is with everyone who is born of the Spirit." This is precisely how the Spirit operates in the world around us. We cannot see His Spiritual form, but we can feel and see His manifestation in the earth.

I called Him during my deepest time of pain and confusion, and He answered me to reveal the hidden things concerning the misunderstood aspects of life, death, and everything in-between. ***"Call to Me, and I will answer you—I will tell you great and hidden things, which you do not know" Jeremiah 33:3.*** He led and guided me every step of the way along this journey, and He ensured that every word was grounded in the truth and principles of the word of God to maintain a mature and seasoned scriptural credibility.

The Holy Spirit descended from Heaven like a mighty rushing wind fifty days after Jesus ascended back to Heaven. Jesus exhorted His apostles that it was better for Him to leave so that the Holy Spirit could come, and they would not be left alone like orphans. The Holy Spirit is here and has been abiding on earth for over 2,000 years. ***"But I tell you the truth, it is to your advantage that I go away! For if I do not go away, the Helper will not come to you; but if I go, I will send Him to you"* John 16:7.**

Albeit, He gave us the Holy Spirit to equip us with His presence and to dwell on the inside of us. He speaks, comforts, teaches, leads, guides, and reveals to us knowledge and truth of all spiritual and earthly matters. Perhaps, you may have never heard of this Holy Spirit, or perhaps you have heard the name but do not understand Him as the person He is. Here are just a few of the scriptural narratives regarding the person and purpose of the Holy Spirit:

John 14:16-18:* *"I will ask the Father, and He will give you another Helper so He may be with you forever—the Spirit of

truth, whom the world cannot receive, because it does not behold Him or know Him. You know Him, because He abides with you and will be in you. I will not abandon you as orphans; I will come to you."

John 14:26: *"But the Helper, the Ruach ha-Kodesh whom the Father will send in My name, will teach you everything and remind you of everything that I said to you."* Ruach ha-Kodesh is the original Hebrew word for the Holy Spirit. *Ruach* alone means Spirit.

Just as God revealed His plans and messages to the Prophets and Apostles, He wants to exhibit Himself to us through the Holy Spirit as the Revealer. *"He reveals deep and hidden things. He knows what lies in darkness and light dwells with Him"* **Daniel 2:22.**

As believers of the gospel, the Holy Spirit functions as the Revealer and will always bear witness to the word of God. The Holy Spirit came to endow the finished work of the Messiah.

John 16:12-15: *"I still have much more to tell you, but you cannot handle it just now. But when the Spirit of truth comes, He will guide you. And He will declare to you the things that are to come. He will glorify Me, because He will take from what is Mine and declare it to you. Everything that the Father has is Mine. For this reason I said the Ruach will take from what is Mine and declare it to you."* Therefore, let's allow the Revealer to help us become cognizant of our afterlife from a biblical delineation, instead of what the world and even other religions have contrived regarding it.

There is a lot of ground and foundation to be laid as we build upon our most holy faith regarding life and death. I will use the Tree of Life Version of the bible unless it is noted otherwise. I

Introduction

personally use this version for its uses of some original Hebraic and Greek words, as well as its translation being by a group of Messianic Rabbis from the Hebrew scriptures in their correct context. I am a full scholar of the total scriptures; therefore, I will also use the Apocrypha Books of the Hebrew Scriptures that were in the original King James Bible in 1611 until removed around 1885 by Saint Jerome, a 4th Century monk that translated the scriptures into Latin. Apocrypha means, "that which is hidden." Furthermore, these were also found as part of the Dead Sea Scrolls about fifty years ago. I will reference Enoch 1, Jubilees, and also the Gospel of Nicodemus, also known as the Acts of Pilate. Peter and Jude in the New Testament referenced 1 Enoch. However, the other three books have riveting hidden messages that will fully connect the dots of many mysteries about life and death. I will share accounts of near-death experiences, including those that were told directly to me from former patients whose names have been changed.

So now that the table has been set, let's sit down, relax, and taste and see that the Lord is good, and His mercy endures forever in Life, Death, and Everything In-Between.

Chapter 1

The Spirit Speaks, Moves, and Reveals.

"I don't want the world to define God for me. I want the Holy Spirit to reveal God to me." ~ Aiden Wilson Tozer

God has bestowed upon the earth the ability to see into the heavenlies that are coexisting simultaneously with us. There is not a thick veil of separation between the two dimensions as our mind's eye envisions or perhaps, we have been led to believe. Understanding the spiritual aspects of death and their components should affect how we live. The coexisting together of spirit, soul, and body occurs on a continuum with the unseen spiritual realms. It is a gift from God when we are allowed to see into this realm, and it is always for a divine purpose when we are granted this gift.

"Let Your will be done on earth as it is in heaven." He desires for Heaven and earth to kiss one another in living and equally so in dying. There is a celestial interdependence between the two dimensions of life. This is one of the great mysteries of God's Kingdom for earth's inhabitants to understand.

I would have never dreamt that my son's unexpected death would produce such a glorious awakening to see the convergence of both. The spiritual realm is the real existence and the earthly one that we perceive as life is a mere mirage existing in the desert of a fallen world. Nonetheless, we seek to gain more knowledge about this provisional state that we call being alive and evade other matters that will help us to be abreast of what we call death.

We refer to death as "the other side" or "crossing over." However, we are not really crossing over or going to the other side. We are merely opening our eyes to its presence that occurs instantaneously at the cessation of vital processes of the body. In reality, the spiritual realm is operating simultaneously with our earthly existence, but our awareness of it is limited. To function as human flesh in a physical environment, we are designed to be bound to this earthly dimension by a physical body. However, God can supersede this physical body and allow the spiritual eyes to see what's commingling with the earthly realm of time and space. When He allows man to "see" the unseen spiritual realm, we must choose to have faith to receive and believe it. This brings to mind one of the great narratives of the prophet Elisha.

In **2 Kings 6:16,** the prophet Elisha was warned by his terrified servant, who was looking at the enormous Syrian army that was surrounding them for an attack. Unphased, Elisha told his servant with confidence, ***"Do not fear, for those who are with us are more than those who are with them."*** Note that the narrative does not say that those in Heaven are more than those who are surrounding them. Those that were existing simultaneously with Elisha's army were from Heaven but not in Heaven. They were present on earth in their created spiritual form, and although they were Heavenly beings positioned on the earth for battle, not everyone could see them. We have unseen heavenly forces that are assigned to us, but just because we can't see them doesn't negate the fact that they are present with us.

This account is one of the many astounding biblical supports that God can allow us to perceive with spiritual eyes while still in the physical body. After his servant's alarm, **"Elisha prayed**

for the eyes of his servant to be opened" to see that which was unseen. *"Then Elisha prayed and said, "ADONAI, please open his eyes that he may see." Then ADONAI opened the eyes of the young man and he saw, and behold, the mountain was full of horses and chariots of fire all around Elisha." 2 Kings 6:17.* God answered Elisha's prayer, and the servant saw the heavenly forces, the horses and chariots of fire surrounding Elisha. Elisha, being full of the Spirit and faith, penetrated the natural veil to see the angelic army surrounding them; therefore, he had no fear but only faith. However, his servant was only looking at what he could see with the natural eyes and was being moved by natural emotions and logic. "They are going to slaughter us!" he must have been thinking when he ran to Elisha. But the Lord answered Elisha's prayer, and the servant saw that not only were they not alone, but those who were on their side greatly outnumbered those who were against them. Just as **Romans 8:31** recalls: *"What then shall we say to these things? If God is for us, who can be against us?" (NKJV).*

Now the skeptics might be led by their own intellects to ascertain, "Well that was in ancient times and doesn't mean that's applicable for us today. After all, miracles and tongues were done away with once the apostles all died." I can understand the skepticism of non-believers, but it's disconcerting that the modern church can be so divided on basic fundamental beliefs, which creates our different denominations. Thus, the deeper doctrines that address miracles, tongues, angels, visions, or God's ability to speak and interact with man, create even a greater divide among Christian believers. Consequently, God recorded in **Malachi 3:6,** *"I am the LORD and I do not change."* I am here to bear witness to this scripture, as someone who has seen into the unseen realms of the spirit; God is timeless and doesn't change His ways. The documentary called,

"Against All Odds: Israel Survives" by Michael Greenspan, gives an awe-inspiring modern day account of Elisha's narrative. During one of the encounters in the war of 1967, the Israeli soldiers were outnumbered by enemy forces. As the enemy troops began to move in closer, they suddenly stopped and started looking up in the sky with fear on their faces, pointing as they said, "Father Abraham!" The leader went back to report to his commander and told him that when they had looked up, they saw Abraham with a league of angels standing behind him with giant swords. In the 20th century, God performed exactly in the same manner as He did in antiquity. We indeed have a living witness from the firsthand account told by an Israeli soldier that was there, that those that are with us are more than those who are against us!

The fulfillment of Joel's prophecy began with the apostles on Shavuot, which is the Hebraic appointed time that celebrated the receiving of the Ten Commandments. But we call it Pentecost, the day the Holy Spirit came upon the apostles. The Prophet Joel proclaimed: *"But this is what was spoken about through the prophet Joel 'And it shall be in the last days,' says God, 'that I will pour out My Ruach on all flesh. Your sons and your daughters shall prophesy, your young men shall see visions, and your old men shall dream dreams. Even on My slaves, male and female, I will pour out My Ruach in those days, and they shall prophesy. And I will give wonders in the sky above and signs on the earth beneath— blood, and fire, and smoky vapor'" Acts 2:17-19.* Therefore, we ascertain that we have not witnessed the full measure until ALL flesh, not just Jewish flesh, manifests these acts.

It is a challenge for many to embrace the possibility of a miraculous phenomenon because of the constraints of our modern educated intellect, especially in Western civilization and scientific mindsets. Unbelief and skepticism are powerful forces that can produce the toughest of critics. After all, only "crazy" or "weird" people believe that God would speak to you or that some type of miraculous spiritual intervention can truly happen, right? Our ideal dramatics is that if God would speak, one must hear the voice of God thundering in the clouds, sounding like Alex Haley or Morgan Freeman, as portrayed by Hollywood's theatrics. But in this present day, many are challenged to believe that the God of the Bible even exists at all. If we do believe that God exists, does He still speak, move, and act on behalf of man?

When we try to define the works of God as limited earthen vessels, we lose the very essence of who He truly is and who we really are. *"The truth which sets men free is the truth which most men fear to accept." ~ Amit Abraham*

But let's relish with enthusiasm that God left us a cliffhanger in the plot of life's journey in **I Corinthians 2:9-10 (NIV)**. *"'What no man has seen, what no ear has heard, and what no human mind has conceived the things God has prepared for those who love him.' These are the things God has revealed to us by the Spirit. The Spirit searches all things, even the deep things of God."* This should invoke a great expectancy and joyful curiosity about the wonderful things that have been prepared for us, so wonderful that it is beyond our human capabilities to envision the grandiose mind of the Savior. When we behold the wonders of nature and every living creature, we only have a glimpse of the fruitfulness of His labor. If He was this spectacular in creating life, would He be any less spectacular in creating life after life? He is not a God that does anything half-heartedly or incompletely.

Jesus left us with the blueprint for our future, and the hope of what is to come after this part of living is done. He said that there were many rooms or places for us to LIVE in His Father's house. The best part is, He is designing and preparing a place uniquely for each one of us, according to our desires. If we have accepted Him and believed in who He is and what He has done for us on the cross, He will come and take us to be with Him when it's our time to depart this life. If we have not, then we will spend all eternity without Him. *"My Father's house has many rooms; if that were not so, would I have told you that I am going there to prepare a place for you? And if I go and prepare a place for you, I will come back and take you to be with me that you also may be where I am" John 14:2-3.*

In these pages lies the spiritual milieu that can only be understood and accepted by the Spirit of God. Before we can understand the realm of the spirit, we must first recognize that God is only reached through our internal spirit man, thus, Spirit to spirit. Our inner spirit must be reborn and endowed by the Holy Spirit. Apostle Paul admonishes us that this Spirit is the same One that raised Jesus from the dead and brings life to our mortal bodies (Romans 8:11 NKJV). In addition, even after we have been born again, we must go a step further and be transformed by renewing the soulish intellect to the word of God. This is not automatic. We MUST read and study His words that He left for us. This includes the word of God about difficult segments of life, like death and suffering. *"Do not be conformed to this world but be transformed by the renewing of your mind, so that you may discern what is the will of God—what is good and acceptable and perfect" Romans 12:2.* Yes, He desires more than anything that we renew our minds about eternal life and the mechanism that will most likely get us there, which is the physical cessation of life.

Now, the true journey begins. We will methodically walk into the culmination of spiritual implications surrounding my son's full spiritual transition from this state of living into the next. Understanding natural transitions are vital to understanding spiritual transitions. My angelic visitation was a physical manifestation that signaled the transitioning of my son, who was on the brink of transitioning from this life.

God has allowed the exceptional recent phenomena of near-death experiences, or NDEs, where experiencers detail their experiences of the other side of death, either Heaven, Hell, or both, after experiencing clinical death. I am not sure why it is called "near death," since there is nothing "near" about it. They were dead with no signs of physical life; some even woke up in the morgue! But if we think that this has all been under the control of man's intellect and abilities, think again. Consequently, I stopped trying to place my experiences in a box that man has a label and classification for, such as an NDE (Near Death Experience), OBE (Out of Body Experience), or SDE (Shared Death Experience). But what I can guarantee is that I had what I will call an MSE—Miraculous Spiritual Encounter. Although research and scientific study have produced terms such as NDE, OBE, and SDE, the reality is that they are all MSEs. There are countless MSEs on record, and the Bible is full of them: Moses, Daniel, Ezekiel, Enoch, Elisha, Jacob, John the Revelator, Paul, and Peter, just to name a few. Whether in our bodies or out, God is in the business of revealing the miraculous.

God has rippled the waters of the hearts and minds of men and women to study and research what happens when this physical life is over. Because of the advanced ability to provide resuscitation, God has allowed mankind to come back with knowledge and experiences that answer the question of the greatest unknown, "What happens when we die?" The Holy Spirit granted the revelation of this mystery. There will be many areas where our knowledge has increased because we have been allowed to run back and forth into the spiritual realms by way of NDE, OBE, SDE, spiritual visitations, or visions and dreams; we have access to its grandeur.

The Holy Spirit brought to my remembrance the account of the angel of the Lord telling Daniel to shut up the words and seal the book until the end times when knowledge will increase. ***"Many shall run to and fro, and knowledge shall increase"* Daniel 12:4 (NIV).** We have never been closer than we are today to the end times. In fact, scientific knowledge is confirming spiritual knowledge. The finding of the Dead Sea Scrolls, hidden in the caves of Qumran, is a perfect example of the moves of God that are allowing knowledge to increase in the end times. There have been nearly 13 million reported NDEs. Yet, there are presumably many more who have never reported their experiences out of fear. In my own transparency, over five years ago, when I first heard of this type of phenomenon occurring, I bore a combination of emotions: being mesmerized, scared, overjoyed, skeptical, but mostly in awe that this has and is happening to people. Being fortunate enough to have any one of these experiences is an ultimate gift; however, it may be tempting to keep it silent and hidden from others out of fear that your own sanity may come into question. *"**Don't be afraid of your fears. They're not there to scare you. They're there to let you know that something is worth it." ~ C. JoyBell.*** There are times that I personally shudder from the vulnerability that comes with revealing my beyond-the-natural experiences (which is what supernatural means) that have occurred in my life. This book is only a glimpse of them as they relate to my son's death.

There are a plethora of books and videos available for anyone interested in this topic. There are some incredible firsthand accounts of testimonies from experiencers who share their stories. We live in a most stupendous age of technology, especially with the development of YouTube™ that serves as a conduit to reach people all over the world with recordings of these encounters. Some of the after-effects for experiencers have been depression and deep displeasure with having to be back on this earth. One experiencer stated that this earth is the dream, and heaven is the only thing that is real. Another person stated that earth was a mirage, and heaven is the real place that we were always meant to be. Many express it as being home. I have added specific accounts of these experiences, based on their relevance, to the remaining chapters.

I'm astounded to share the supernatural encounters surrounding my son's death and seeing him stand before Jesus on the other side. I witnessed his decision and choice to stay departed from this life. It was designed by God for me to have had this unique experience that bears some resemblance to many aspects of an NDE. However, this was not an NDE because I did not experience any type of clinical death. Through this experience, I hope to solidify and shift the mindset about how we view death. Through the countless NDEs that I listened to, it became the confirmation that served to answer so many different aspects of my experiences. According to Deuteronomy, with three witnesses a matter will stand and two witnesses can provide conclusive proof of reality. However, one witness alone cannot serve as a reliable source to the truth of a matter.

I have tested and tried all experiences and insight by weighing them only by the word of God as my first and second witnesses. My third witness is several different testimonies from others firsthand accounts of near-death experiences and books of Heaven and Hell encounters. Satan was created in heaven as one of God's chief angels; he possesses full knowledge of Heaven's functioning and, most of all, God's Holy Word. Believe this! He knows how to counterfeit anything that is of God's Kingdom. Satan was not satisfied to just become equal to or like God, but he wanted to be exalted ABOVE the Most High God. The biblical account of Jesus' temptation by Satan in the wilderness, found in the ***Gospel of Matthew 4:1-11***, exhibited his knowledge of God's word, and He quoted it to Jesus. He strived to tempt Jesus with wealth and power by giving Him all the kingdoms in the world if He would just bow down and worship him. This was and still is his main objective; to be worshipped like his Creator, our Creator.

An ominous characteristic of a demonic disguised angelic being as opposed to a true angelic being from God is the demonstration of self-exaltation or request for worship. We will come back to this in greater detail shortly. When Jesus was tempted by the devil in the wilderness after fasting 40 days and nights, Jesus replied to him, "Go Satan! For it is written, **'YOU SHALL WORSHIP THE LORD YOUR GOD AND SERVE HIM ONLY!'"** Satan MASQUERADES as an angel of light and goodness. This is to lure in an unsuspecting individual into deception like he did with Eve. ***2 Corinthians 11:14: "And no wonder, for even Satan masquerades as an angel of light".*** He wants us to see him as we see GOD—good, full of love, and truth. He makes things appear as if it's coming from The Light of the World, because if he appeared in the likeness of the darkness and cruelty that he really is, he wouldn't be appealing. If we expect him to appear with horns and a pitchfork, then we need to think again. For this appearance would immediately disclose the satanic realms of his existence and leave little room for deception.

The Spirit Speaks, Moves, and Reveals.

We are to test the spirits to see if they are of God or not. I John 4:1-3 tells us: *"Beloved, do not believe every spirit, but test the spirits to see whether they are from God, for many false prophets have gone out into the world. By this you know the Spirit of God: every spirit that confesses that Jesus Christ has come in the flesh is from God, and every spirit that does not confess Jesus is not from God. This is the spirit of the antichrist, which you heard was coming and now is in the world already."*

Two 14th century well known occultists, named John Dee and Sir Edward Kelly, were summoning and communing with entities of the spirit world that they believed to be angels. This was done with full knowledge and support of Queen Elizabeth I. Dee and Kelly were both considered to be believers in Jesus Christ and part of the Catholic church. Although the "angels" were initially speaking spiritual sounding religious rhetoric about Jesus under the guises of Gabriel, Uriel, and Raphael, one evening the men had been told that they would be given a vital secret. The angel of light pulled back the dark cloak of deception and revealed himself through his words. The antichrist spirit was on full display with the doctrine of demons that: Jesus was not God; no one should pray to Him; there's no such thing as sin; creation of man was not true; angels do not accept anything about the Holy Spirit; and there's immortal life through reincarnation. Kelly feared that they had now been summoning demons and he was correct. He left his work with Dee.

If we are not filled with the Spirit, we cannot test the spirits. We must be confident in knowing the character of God to avoid the pitfalls of deception. Jesus even warns that in the last day, many will come and proclaim that they are Christ and will do signs and wonders, but He warns us not to fall into the false delusions. His foretelling of the specific events that will signal the last days before

His coming culminates when the last trumpet will sound and we see Him coming in the clouds. Additionally, God implores that NO MAN, not even Christ Himself, knows the exact time of His return. ***Matthew 24:36-37: "But concerning that day and hour no one knows, not even the angels of heaven, nor the Son, but the Father only. For as were the days of Noah, so will be the coming of the Son of Man."***

Consequently, many cults and false religions have been framed with the belief that its leader has predicted the day of His return. However, when the day did not produce a coming Messiah, they simply spun a reason and/or came up with another date. I draw the conclusion that it is imperative to learn and understand the scriptures for ourselves. **2 Timothy 2:15 (KJV)** admonishes us to ***"Study to shew thyself approved unto God, a workman that needeth not to be ashamed, rightly dividing the word of truth."*** Let's rightly divide the word truth about angels, false religion, and spiritualism in the next chapters.

Chapter 2

Beware of Angels

"Insight is better than eyesight when it comes to seeing an angel."~ Eileen Elias Freeman

During my grappling with my experiences and conducting much research about life, death, and angels, I reviewed a riveting documentary entitled, *Beware of Angels, Deception in the Last Days*. I was intrigued by that title and thinking, *Why should I beware of angels?* It's based on the book by the late Roger Morneau, who was a former member of the occult. He had become a born-again Christian after attending a series of bible studies with a co-worker and his wife. The story was also featured on one the episodes called *The Naked Truth* in the series entitled *Twisted Sisters* on *Investigation Discovery*. The events are recounted mainly by Sharon's son, who was twelve at the time, and the deceased victim's surviving spouse.

It is one of the most disturbing stories that I've ever read. There were two sisters, infamously referred to as the Halsted Sisters, that were part of a Seventh Day Adventist Bible study group of nineteen members who prayed to see angels. Unlike John Dee and Edward Kelly, these church members were not attempting to engage in the occult. Nonetheless, it produced the same results with far more sinister overt consequences of murder. Moving on, the request to see angels was granted but they were not from Heaven and they were not from God! The youngest Halstead son began channeling at seven-years old and giving messages to the group. By the age of nine, he was alleged to have received the message from the angels to kill the Green family. This was a perfect example of the danger in summoning any entity in the second heaven, where spiritual principalities and demons reside. As the old saying goes, "Be careful what you ask for because you just may get it."

Over a few years, they had recorded interactions with over 160 different angels. One of the principal angels that did the most interacting with the group was named Naked Truth. This should have produced a flashing red light all over the place, wouldn't you agree? The angels' names that we do know of from our Biblical text are Micha**el**, Gabri**el**, Rapha**el**, and Uri**el**. Note that each of these names ends in El, which translates to *God* or *deity* in Hebrew. God is **El-ohim**, The Creator, as seen in Genesis. The name Naked Truth bears full resemblance to the pride and carnality of the god of this world, Satan. Moreover, according to their written accounts with the angels, the angels were saturated with self-exaltation and boastings of their powers and abilities. The angel, Naked Truth, made inflammatory claims that he possessed all of the answers and his words were the same as Jesus' words. But similar to the account of Dee and Kelly, the demonic entities go in for the kill and inform the group that they no longer need Jesus as a mediator. They elevated the group's minds by further telling them that they will hear things directly for themselves and will see many glorious things.

Once the blasphemous statement was heard that there was no need for Jesus to be a mediator, this should have immediately stopped all mysticism and opened their eyes to the truth of who they had been entertaining, as Edward Kelly did with the "angelic" testimony that Jesus was not the Son of God. I Timothy 2:5-6 (NIV) declares, "*For there is one God and one mediator between God and mankind, the man Christ Jesus, who gave himself as a ransom for all people. This has now been witnessed to at the proper time.*" The angels knew how to throw in a little scripture and Jesus' name to keep the group believing in them. One of the main foundations of believing in Christ is that He is our mediator. He is the only way that we can be reconciled to the Father God.

There is ALWAYS humility with God's messengers. Most importantly, they would never seek to be worshipped or exalted. "*I, John, am the one who heard and saw these things. And when I heard and saw, I fell down to worship at the feet of the angel who showed me these things. But he said to me, 'Do not do that. I am a fellow servant of yours and of your brethren the prophets and of those who heed the words of this book. Worship God'*" *Revelation 22:8-9.*

The Word of God instructs us to never pray to or show any form of worship to angels. Many people have fallen into angel worship, and God warns against it. "*Let no one rob you of your prize by a voluntary humility and worshipping of the angels, dwelling in the things which he has not seen, vainly puffed up by his fleshly mind*" **Colossians 2:18 (WEB).**

The New Age philosophies have promoted Angel Numbers as a form of angelic communication to us. It is a complete smokescreen of deception by Satan and deceives people into believing they are achieving higher forms of spirituality and power.

It pains me to the core to think about how many people believe they are achieving a higher spiritual level by participating in this form of mysticism and are completely unaware that they are only opening their souls to demonic activity. There are numerous testimonies of those who were once bound by new age religion and the occult, such as Roger Morneau, that have shed a great light of truth about whose authority these practices are committed through, and it's not God!

The members had written that one of the "bright beings" was Jesus, and he told them that they need to follow this angel and obey all that he tells them. Jesus would never instruct anyone to follow an angel. He said that while on earth that He obeyed and said only what The Father told Him to do, not angels.

"But even if we (or an angel from heaven) should announce any 'good news' to you other than what we have proclaimed to you, let that person be cursed! As we have said before, so I now repeat: if anyone proclaims to you 'good news' other than what you received, let that person be under a curse!" Galatians 1:8-9.

Again, it's imperative to stack every word and experience against the word of God.

The members would ask to see the angels, and they would manifest to them. God's heavenly beings only obey Him, and they would not physically appear at any given moment at our request or summoning. **Luke 4:10. "For it is written, 'He will command His angels concerning you, to guard you.'"** Angels hearken the instructions and command of the Lord, not us. Even in times of distress, we should only call on the name of the Lord, who has the authority to send His messengers to help us.

The Bible study group possessed notebooks composed of all of the angelic encounters with them and mentioned gifts, such as golden slippers from heaven given to them by Sam, one of the angels. Sam was one of the false angels. But we know that it is the Lord who hides us under the shadow of His wings, and He lifts us up by the power of His mighty hand. The demonic entities had bestowed such an extent of great power on the members that they were able to go into stores and steal televisions and VCRs completely undetected as if they were invisible. They would walk right out the front door carrying the stolen merchandise. It was these acts of theft that caused the Green family to determine that something was not right with these so-called angelic encounters and leave the group. The angels had some of the members practice astral projection.

Satan tempted Jesus with the wealth of all of the kingdoms of this world, and he still entices people with power and wealth today. For that is what man craves the most. The fall of Adam and Eve was essentially the desire to have power over themselves, and it cost them their very lives, just as God told them that it would.

Unfortunately, the most disturbing and bone-chilling command of the angel, Naked Truth, resulted in a great tragedy. Two sisters were told to shoot several members who had left the group, including a husband, wife, and their three-year-old son, which started their murder spree. Sadly, the wife died, but the husband and son survived physically. The husband was alive, but he wasn't able to truly live for a while due to his grief, fear, and depression. He was initially unable to take care of his son, who was paralyzed from the neck down as a result of the shooting.

When the sisters were asked by the prosecutor their motive for their crimes, they replied, *"The angel told us to do it!"* At this point, they had become extremely fearful of the angels' threats, and the true character of darkness was being revealed beyond the masqueraded angels of light. The two sisters stated that they felt they had no choice. The angel, Naked Truth, threatened that if they did not commit the murders, they would become "totaled," which meant the spirit or immortal soul is no longer in the person's body, and that person no longer exists; therefore, they are fully demon-possessed. *"This man no longer exists. That which he was born, died and only the enemy remains [demons]"* This was the motive for the murders. The angel told them six people were totaled and needed to be destroyed; that family had been a part of this group.

These members fell into the devil's trap of pride and power. These are the things in his arsenal that he uses to tempt us. In this case, the ladies succumbed to them, and that turned into stealing, killing, and destroying—the epitome of Satan's full character. There is nothing new that Satan can do or try, no new tricks in the bag of schemes. It all has been done before; as Ecclesiastes tells us, there is nothing new under the sun.

Through His examples, Christ showed us how to defeat the devil. We must know the word, speak the word, and resist him. If we do these things, he will flee! Let's be aware of how he operates, as **1 Peter 5:8** instructs us: **"Be sober [well balanced and self-disciplined], be alert and cautious at all times. That enemy of yours, the devil, prowls around like a roaring lion [fiercely hungry], seeking someone to devour" (AMP).**

How sorrowful that what started out as a group of innocent people studying the Bible together ended up in a horrific tragedy because of the enemy's deception. Be that as it may, the real tragedy is studying the Bible and not having the spiritual discernment to recognize what is of God's character and what is not. It's more disconcerting that they were part of a religious group that upholds the Ten Commandments to the point that they worship on Saturday to "remember the Sabbath Day and Keep It Holy." Yet, they disobeyed so many more commandments, such as "Thou Shall Not Steal," "Thou Shall Not Kill," and "Thou Shall Have No Other Gods."

It is a matter of spiritual life or death that we must use the word of God to rightly judge every experience with discernment by the Holy Spirit. If you don't know the true characteristics of God and the Holy Spirit, then beware of angels!

Chapter 3

Put Away the Impure Princes of False Religion

"Now the Holy Spirit tells us clearly that in the last times some will turn away from the true faith; they will follow deceptive spirits and teachings that come from demons." ~ I Timothy 4:1

The most common motive for seeking out psychics and mediums is grief. The desire to have "contact" with the deceased loved one weighs on the heart and mind, which results in seeking out those who practice this form of supernatural ability. Sadly, I have heard numerous opinions from Christian believers who believe there's nothing wrong or sinful about the practice of seeking the dead, using psychics, or even being a medium. Furthermore, I have noted that many survivors of near-death experiences or out-of-body experiences seem to turn to mysticism at some level, even proclaiming themselves as mediums and believing they are operating with God's help. It's as if the confines of this meager earth become so dissatisfying, and they try to have a foothold in both worlds, but mainly the world that was more vivid and real. But the testimony of God's word is clear! ***"Do not turn to mediums, necromancers; do not seek them out, and so make yourselves unclean by them: I am the Lord your God" Leviticus 19:31 (ESV).***

God is not schizophrenic, nor is He a hypocrite! He would not command us to shun these practices and then turn around and be the source to help us do them. But this was precisely what King Saul did. But before we examine Saul's account, let's further examine necromancy in detail. Note the following definition:

Necromancy is a practice of magic involving communication with the dead – either by summoning their spirit as an apparition or raising them bodily – for the purpose of divination, imparting the means to foretell future events or discover hidden knowledge, to bring someone back from the dead, or to use the dead as a weapon, as the term may sometimes be used in a more general sense to refer to black magic or witchcraft.

An additional scripture in **Deuteronomy 18:9-13 (ESV)** says, **"When you come into the land that the Lord your God is giving you, you shall not learn to follow the abominable practices of those nations. There shall not be found among you anyone who burns his son or his daughter as an offering, anyone who practices divination or tells fortunes or interprets omens, or a sorcerer or a charmer or a medium or a necromancer or one who inquires of the dead, for whoever does these things is an abomination to the Lord."**

Now let's recall the narrative of King Saul as he summons the prophet Samuel from the dead. The Holy Spirit had already departed from Saul because of his disobedience. So out of desperation, he chose to disobey further by going to a necromancer. But Saul was very double-minded because he had previously removed all of the mediums in the land. *I Samuel 25:3*: "*Saul had expelled the mediums and spiritists from the land.*" Let's continue on to the historical narrative.

I Samuel 28:5-20: "*Saul took one look at the Philistine army and started shaking with fear. So he asked the Lord what to do. But the Lord would not answer, either in a* dream or by a priest or a prophet. Then Saul told his officers, 'Find me a woman who can talk to the spirits of the dead. I'll go to her and find out what's going to happen.'

His servants told him, 'There's a woman at Endor who can talk to spirits of the dead.'

That night, Saul put on different clothing so nobody would recognize him. Then he and two of his men went to the woman, and asked, 'Will you bring up the ghost of someone for us?'

The woman said, 'Why are you trying to trick me and get me killed? You know King Saul has gotten rid of everyone who talks to the spirits of the dead!'

Saul replied, 'I swear by the living Lord that nothing will happen to you because of this.'

'Who do you want me to bring up?' she asked.

'Bring up the ghost of Samuel,' he answered.

When the woman saw Samuel, she screamed. Then she turned to Saul and said, 'You've tricked me! You're the king!'

'Don't be afraid,' Saul replied. 'Just tell me what you see.'

She answered, 'I see a spirit rising up out of the ground.'

'What does it look like?'

'It looks like an old man wearing a robe.'

Saul knew it was Samuel, so he bowed down low.

'Why are you bothering me by bringing me up like this?' Samuel asked.

'I'm terribly worried,' Saul answered. 'The Philistines are about to attack me. God has turned his back on me and won't answer any more by prophets or by dreams. What should I do?'

Samuel said, 'If the Lord has turned away from you and

is now your enemy, don't ask me what to do. I've already told you: The Lord has sworn to take the kingdom from you and give it to David. And that's just what he's doing! When the Lord was angry with the Amalekites, he told you to destroy them, but you didn't do it. That's why the Lord is doing this to you. Tomorrow the Lord will let the Philistines defeat Israel's army, then you and your sons will join me down here in the world of the dead.'

At once, Saul collapsed and lay stretched out on the floor, terrified at what Samuel had said. He was weak because he had not eaten."

Pagans had a legitimate practice as a profession of summoning the dead. But God forbade the Israelites, His people that were set apart from other nations, to avoid such practices. That transfers to us, who are grafted in with His chosen people, because it was a principle that He set, and a principle does not change. Please do not be misled. Many believe that their supernatural gifts are from God. But IF they use any of the aforementioned sources, they are not functioning with the power and help from God. Let's be clear: I didn't state that what they were seeing or hearing was not real. Understand that there are real manifestations that come from dark principalities and powers. The modern term is "white magic" vs. "black magic." Recall when Moses was contending with Pharaoh's magicians? Moses threw down his staff, and it turned into a snake, but so did the magicians' staffs. However, Moses' snake swallowed up the magicians' staffs as a demonstration that God reigned supreme over the enemy's counterfeits and devices.

"Adonai told Moses and Aaron, 'When Pharaoh speaks to you saying, "Prove yourselves with a miracle," then you are to say to Aaron, 'Take your staff and cast it down before Pharaoh,

so that it may become a serpent.'

"*So Moses and Aaron went into Pharaoh and did as Adonai had commanded. Aaron threw down his staff before Pharaoh and before his servants, and it became a serpent. Then Pharaoh called for the wise men and the sorcerers, and they too, the magicians of Egypt, did the same with their secret arts. For each man threw down his staff, and they became serpents. But Aaron's staff swallowed up their staffs. Yet Pharaoh's heart was hardened. So he did not listen to them—just as Adonai had said" Exodus 7:8-13.*

Some men and women use the power of darkness to perform false signs and wonders, yet the signs and wonders are real. I know that sounds like an oxymoron to say that the false signs are real. But this was exactly the premise of the narrative of Moses versus the magicians. In as much as the manifestations are real, the source behind them is false because it is not of God but Satan. I beseech and urge anyone who credits themselves a psychic, medium, or spiritualist to be pricked in your heart by the truth about these practices. There are true giftings that the Holy Spirit has given God's people, but they would never violate His DIVINE word. "***Sanctify them in the truth; your word is truth" I Timothy 3:16 (ESV).*** My brother and sister, my hope is that you will be sanctified in the truth of God's word about this issue.

Chapter 4

Messages from Heaven

"Love is stronger than death even though it can't stop death from happening, but no matter how hard death tries it can't separate people from love. It can't take away our memories either. In the end, life is stronger than death."~ Unknown

I know from personal experience that there are supernatural experiences that science cannot explain, and I have embraced the coined phrase, *Exceptional Human Experiences (EHE)*.

There is a new concept called *After Death Communication* or *ADC*, a phrase originating from the book called *Hello from Heaven*. ADC is where a loved one will communicate to you after their death through various means, such as their fragrance suddenly filling up the room or feeling a touch or a hug from an invisible source, to let you know they are there. But most notably are visions of the loved one appearing or speaking to you through lucid dreams. I will share my own personal experiences of what can be "classified" as an ADC. This is completely different from Necromancy and seeking to summon or speak to the dead.

I want to be VERY clear. I do not want the lines to get blurred about this particular subject. Again, I do not support the use of channeling, mysticism, or necromancy of any kind. This is not about overt communicating with the dead with the belief that dead loved ones can be summoned or come back in a spiritual form at will or even your will to commune with you. However, do I believe God can allow some exceptional human experiences to occur in some form that is within His sovereignty & guidelines? Yes! I based this on the biblical knowledge that God allowed Moses and Elijah to come and speak to Jesus in the account of the transfiguration on the mountain in Matthew 17:2. This is in stark contrast to the account of Saul, who enlisted a known medium and necromancer to summon up the spirit of the Prophet Samuel. Saul sinned! God cannot sin, so whatever HE allows to transcend by His divine ordinance, such as communicating through lucid dreams, is in the confines of His history in dealing with man. If He can send an angel to speak to Joseph in a dream to get up and flee to Egypt, why couldn't he send the spirit of a loved one to speak to you in a dream? This is not implying that any or all dreams of a deceased loved one are orchestrated by God. We dream naturally as a part of sleeping. But there's a distinct difference between the two. With divine dreams, they do not quickly fade, if ever, unlike normal "pizza dreams." So now that we have established these merits, let's continue on.

My best friend and stepmother, Amelia Lee Machen, born March 18, 1956, left us on May 10, 2009, which was Mother's Day that year. I will never forget it. I was sitting in church, and they were just handing out white roses to members who had lost their mothers when I received my brother's text that read, "she's gone." The gripping pain numbed my whole body. I had a flight booked already, due to getting the news that she was declining, and this made it even more heartbreaking that I didn't get to tell her goodbye personally. She was the best person in the entire world.

The days and months were just unbearable at times. I even attempted to move to Houston, Texas to be with my younger brother and sister to try in some way to be there to "help" them through this, but I wasn't able to help them because I couldn't help myself. I could remember visiting her resting place one evening alone, trying to grasp the reality of her death.

After several months, I began to have a series of dreams about her that were spread over a period of approximately four months. Although I can't recall many of the conversations or events, I can still remember the very last dream. In that dream, she told me that she could no longer come to visit me and that everything was going to be okay. This dream was much more detailed and vivid, but due to some very personal matters involving other family members, I will only share that particular part. It's been ten years, and I have never forgotten this one dream. I have not had any lucid dreams about her since that very last one. Was that a coincidence that she said that she could no longer come to me anymore, and she didn't, or was it an Exceptional Human Experience of After Death Communication?

When my son passed away, I had a very lucid dream about him, and it was so real! He sat on my bed, and I had asked him a question that I had wondered about, known only between God and me. He sat down beside me on my bed, wearing a yellow shirt with blue letters. We had a sweet conversation, and it was so moving and felt so real that as I was beginning to arouse, I reached out my hand to feel him sitting on the side of my bed, only to find that he was not there. The joy but then sadness was intertwined and very tangible. I still felt his presence. This was the first lucid dream of our ADC. About five months later, I was cleaning through the closet, and there were two of the same shirts that he was wearing the night he came to me. My heart froze inside my chest as I clutched his shirt in my hand and deeply inhaled his scent.

The next experience that I had was way more complex and captivating, although I still can't explain this EHE. I will discuss in another chapter about transitions that occur before someone has died, but for now, I need to display one aspect of his transition that applies to this particular subject matter.

Three months before my son died, we had the pleasure of having him celebrate my birthday with his sisters and me. I was so excited to have my son home. The kids had gotten me a birthday card, and everyone signed it. Honestly, among the shuffle of things, I wasn't sure where the card was. However, on my birthday the following nine months after he passed, I was still severely broken in despair and grief. My girls attempted to make me feel better by giving me a little birthday celebration, but although I was very appreciative of their efforts, we all couldn't help but cry as we remembered that he was just with us for my last birthday.

As the night came to an end and everyone went back home, I had finished the final steps of the cleanup and had turned off all the lights, locked the doors, and was en route to my bedroom when my foot slid across something on the floor. I was completely shocked because the house was spotless, and I had just vacuumed and knew that it would have been impossible to miss this rather large object of paper on the floor. So, I bent down to pick it up with a bit of frustration. While holding it in my hand, I saw that it was an older appearing birthday card and was not any of the ones that I had been given that night. I walked into my bedroom and sat down on the bed to look at it more carefully. As soon as I opened it, right at the top of the card was written, "Your son," and signed with his signature. I sat there, confused and astonished. How, who, where did this come from? I couldn't understand how this birthday card from nine months ago appeared at that precise moment, on that exact day, at the precise place that my foot just landed. No one would ever be able to explain this to me. There is no scientific or human intellectual reasoning that would be able to satisfy me with an answer. It is the unexplained moments that God can grant to us that serves as a beacon of light that shows us that He is real and He will respond to every facet of our lives. I can't say if God allowed my son's spiritual body to place it there or an angel placed it there or Jesus Himself placed it there. All I knew was, it was there! I called all of my girls and asked them if they saw it earlier or had it that night and left it there and no one had. They were just as bewildered and mystified as I was. This experience was truly a Hello from Heaven. I wept ferociously from the joy of feeling His love. When I say His, I'm speaking of the Lord. The fact that He allowed such an incredible gift, regardless of the how, who, where, or when it occurred, I felt him, my son, saying "Happy Birthday, Mom" and Him, my Savior saying, "I see you and I feel your pain. I love you so much and I worked this moment for you to let you know you are not forgotten."

I have heard many Experiencers, that give their testimony about going to Heaven, speak about how birthdays, weddings, and births are witnessed by our deceased loved ones. One lady explained that there are portals that our deceased loved ones can go to and look down at their loved ones anytime, but especially these significant events. Another Experiencer explained that angels, as well as other recently deceased loved ones that arrive, will tell our family members what had occurred on the earth before they arrived. I will not dispute this possibility because I know what I have experienced personally along this journey that has made me a believer in the unbelievable!

Chapter 5

If There's a Heaven, There Must Be a Hell

On a tombstone, our birth and death are separated with a dash. The dash represents the in-between from the point of our beginning and the point of our ending. Etched into the granite is the exact date of our birth and our death. But within the dash, what else did your life stand for? There is a difference between what you accomplished and what your life stood for. You could be a millionaire, but did you stand for love, joy, peace, patience, kindness, goodness, faithfulness, gentleness, and self-control, which is the fruit of the Spirit of God? ***"But the fruit of the Ruach is love, joy, peace, patience, kindness, goodness, faithfulness, gentleness, and self-control—against such things there is no law" Galatians 5:22-23. In addition***, did your life offer compassion, mercy, humility, and justice for the poor and needy? We will take a deep dive into how this life will measure against your life-after-life in a few short chapters.

However, contained within the dash between your life and death should be the most important date of all. Although it is invisible on the granite, it is forever etched in the spiritual tablet of the Lamb's Book of Life. The dash should hold our spiritual rebirth into the family and the Kingdom of God. This is our second birthday and the one that will end up counting the most, as it is the complete prerequisite for whether we have a third. The third and final birthday is actually our date of transition that we call death. If we celebrate the second birthday of the reborn spirit, then we get to walk into the land of our happily-ever-after in the presence of Almighty God and partake of our third final rebirth of life-after-life. Otherwise, instead of the second birthday of being born again, we will have the second and final death. Allow me to expound upon this with great clarity.

"If I never spoke of hell, I should think I had kept back something that was profitable, and should look on myself as an accomplice of the devil."- J. C. Ryle. I am required to acknowledge this sensitive but necessary segment of the afterlife.

"When I say to the wicked: 'Wicked one, you will surely die!' and you do not speak to warn the wicked about his way—that wicked one will die in his iniquity, but his blood I will require at your hand. If you warn the wicked of his way to turn from it and he does not turn from his way, then he will die in his iniquity—but you have saved your soul" Ezekiel 33:8-9. We are reforming our thought processes about death and life-after-life; however, I cannot do this without warning of the consequences of not accepting Christ as Lord and Savior.

Death never equals annihilation, meaning no longer existing at all. We all are going to live forever, either in Heaven or Hell. But if someone ends up "living" forever in Hell, this is called the second death because that soul and spirit will never stop existing, feeling, and being fully conscious and aware of its eternal death. ***"But for the cowardly and faithless and detestable and murderers and sexually immoral and sorcerers and idolaters and all liars— their lot is in the lake that burns with fire and brimstone, which is <u>the second death.</u>"*** But there will be no fruits of life such as joy, love, and peace with eternal bliss of the glorious finished work that Jesus did for us on the cross.

This is the only true death that exists. I know that sounds a bit ludicrous for any of us that have suffered through the pain and despair of losing a loved one, but please stay with me.

This universe is based on equal and opposite reactions such as hot/cold, up/down, backward/forward, good/bad, righteous/evil. So, therefore, how could we choose to believe that there is Heaven but not Hell? There is a false narrative placed in the minds of men by Satan himself that there is no Hell, just as he deceived Adam and Eve into believing that they would surely not die if they ate from the forbidden tree. *"You are of your father the devil, and you want to do the desires of your father. He was a murderer from the beginning and does not stand in the truth, because there is no truth in him. Whenever he speaks lies he is just being himself—for he is a liar and the father of lies" John 8:44.* Satan speaks to our soul all things that are contrary to the Word and character of God. When he speaks, it is a lie. There is no truth in him.

First and foremost, Hell was NEVER created for man. It was only created for the Devil and both sets of fallen angels. *"Then He will also say to those on the left, 'Go away from Me, you cursed ones, into the everlasting fire which has been prepared for the devil and his angels" Matthew 25:41.* After Satan caused man to fall, this created a vast chasm between God and man. What fellowship does light have with darkness? This division voided eternal life and fellowship with God. The Garden of Eden was perfection without want or need. Father, Son, and Holy Spirit walked in the cool of the day with them. Satan thought that he could contrive the installation of death as a laughable moment to put an end to the creation that was made in the image of God. Man was the only being that could claim this divine distinction of being created in the image of God.

But the redemption of man was already set in the hearts and minds of the Father, Son, and the Holy Spirit before the foundation of the world was laid. The Three were in one accord because They are One, yet each played a separate part. If it wasn't for the Son, who came to the earth in flesh and blood to sacrifice Himself, Jews and Gentiles would not have had the chance for salvation and would have ended up in the abode of the dead in Sheol for all eternity.

I am sure you have heard or perhaps even said it yourselves. "How could a loving God send anyone to Hell?" It is imperative to acknowledge that God didn't choose Hell for us; we do because we are free-will beings, just as Adam and Eve were. Our rejection of the gospel is our decision to accept Hell. *"The Lord is not slow in keeping his promise, as some people think of slowness; on the contrary, he is patient with you; for it is not his purpose that anyone should be destroyed, but that everyone should turn from his sins" 2 Peter 3:9 (CJB).* He went to the depths of the earth to save us, literally.

There have been many recorded accounts of people's experiences seeing hell. They saw hell either through an NDE or God merely taking them in a vision or a real experience of temporarily releasing their spirit from the body without a clinical death and seeing this domain as Mary K. Baxter experienced. The devil loves to defraud us into believing that Hell doesn't exist. I am not a gambling person, but if I wanted to roll the dice on what is truth and what is false, I am going to bet on what I have the least to lose and most to gain. So, I'd much rather believe in Hell and do all I can to not go there than to believe that there isn't one and do the very things that can get me there, only to find out that it's real. *"I would rather live my life as if there is a God and die to find out there isn't, than live as if there isn't and to die to find out there is." Albert Camus.*

Therefore, I would choose to lose everything in order to trade everlasting death for eternal life. ***"Do not be afraid of those who kill the body but cannot kill the soul. Rather, be afraid of the One who can destroy both soul and body in hell" Matthew 10:28 (NIV)***. So, if hell destroys both soul and body, then this must imply that Heaven would do the complete opposite, correct? The soul and spiritual body will be maintained through eternal life until the Lord returns to earth again. Then our earthly bodies will rise and reconnect to our spiritual bodies into a newer glorified body because we will be inhabiting the New Earth. We will expound on this in greater detail when we get the pleasure to explore more about Heaven.

Hell is a REAL PLACE and NOT a "state of mind" or "symbolism" of being separated from God, although there is a literal separation from God's presence for all eternity. There are horrific things that occur in the physical place of Hell! In Mary K. Baxter's book, *A Divine Revelation of Hell*, Chapter 1, she describes the indescribable horrors of Hell. She warns that our souls will live forever, and she urges everyone to not come to this real place of torment. It is easy for Satan to convince people that her and many others' experiences are not true because no one wants to believe it. It's frightening and sets our soul on a path of great uneasiness at just the thought that there's another option to this life's end other than the joy and beauty of Heaven. When we choose death over life, we crucify Jesus all over again. What pain and anguish this brings the Savior to have to see any of His creation decide to forsake their life and salvation that is freely given. ***"'Do I delight at all in the death of the wicked?' It is a declaration of Adonai. 'Rather, should he not return from his ways, and live?'" Ezekiel 18:23 (NKJV)***. Just as God pleaded with Israel, so He pleads with us today. ***"Say to them: 'As I live'—it is a declaration of Adonai— 'I have no pleasure in the death of the wicked, but that the wicked turn from his way and live. Return, return from your evil ways. Why will you die, O house of Israel?'" Ezekiel 33:11.*** This is an unambiguous precept in scripture. HE DOES NOT TAKE PLEASURE IN ANYONE LOSING THEIR LIFE IN HELL, PERIOD! This is not to be used as a scare tactic but as a just weight to balance the scales of life and death with ALL of the truth in God's word. ***"Hell is the highest reward that the devil can offer you for being a servant of his."- Billy Sunday.*** This quote sums up the totality of this segment.

When Yeshua, Jesus, died, the three days before He rose again, He went to Hell for us and took our place. Being one with His Father, there was never a separation between them because He was with the Father God from the beginning. Our sins caused His soul and spirit to be brought down into the heart of the earth. **Matthew 12:40 (NIV)** says, ***"For as Jonas was three days and three nights in the whale's belly; so shall the Son of man be three days and three nights in the heart of the earth."*** We know that Hell is in the heart of the earth. I've heard people say that Hell is here on earth, and that is partly true. It's a physical and spiritual dwelling in the middle and heart of the depths of the earth. Keep in mind that the fallen angels sinned on the earth and were put in chains and outer darkness on the earth. We experience hellish, bad, and tragic events on the earth, but this dimension of earth that we can see with our eyes is not Hell. It seems fitting for this to be where I reveal God's purpose for allowing me to see spiritually what happened when my son crossed over.

My son had been born again in his teenage years, but he didn't grow into maturity in the things of Christ. He had a lot of struggles throughout his life with many issues. He had a season of questioning God because he was very put off and turned off by Christians and their "Christianity," in particular judgmentalism toward everyone and everything without showing the love of Jesus to restore and heal broken people. Judgmentalism never ministers to anyone, and Christ left us with stern warnings about its practices in the Church, and the modern Church is dying because of it. However, he went through a time of restoration and refreshing of reading the word of God and even listening to gospel music. He would send me songs from YouTube that he was so excited about. He and his roommate started attending a Wednesday night Bible study, and I was over the moon. But one evening, he called to tell me how he became completely upset by the prosperity/celebrity-like actions of the pastors of the congregation. He was looking for the real people of God who loved the rich and the poor alike. He was full of so much love and kindness towards others and had a heart bigger than life. He was a brother to his sisters and friends, a loving grandson, and, most of all, an adorable son to me, his mom. During this spiritual renewal, he met a young lady whom he felt deeply about for the first time in many years since the breakup of his high school/college girlfriend. However, after about six months of dating, she died unexpectedly in her sleep at just 21 years old.

This caused him to be confused and angry with God, and it sent him spiraling with questions about the goodness and love of God, not in general but specifically God's love for him. Although he had just recently had this experience with the Lord, he was now being attacked in his mind by Satan.

However, based on implanted religious thinking and dogma, I would have "judged" that he went to Hell because of these shortcomings in his life and not looking like a cookie-cutter

Christian that "we" determine as righteous and worthy of Heaven. This would have definitely compounded my grief, and My Father knew this! God doesn't make quick snap judgments out of anger to throw His children into Hell. The key is, we are ALL His children! But not all of His children, chose to believe in Him. John 5:24 says, **"Truly, truly, I say to you, whoever hears My word and believes Him who sent Me has eternal life. He does not come into judgment, but has passed from death to life."**

In several NDEs, there have been the complete opposite outcomes of how we are taught about who and why someone would go to Hell. At the time of this writing, I had four instances of being personally told first-hand accounts of patient NDEs. Two of them went to Heaven, and two of them went to Hell. One patient, whom I will call Patricia, had a Near Death Experience after the rupture of two brain aneurysms. She shared her experience with me freely, without any knowledge that I was writing this book.

She recounted her experience with great zeal and clarity as she pointed out that she could remember it just like it was yesterday, although it occurred several years ago. She described how she was taken to the very gates of Hell, and she could see the fire in the distance, but yet it was pure blackness at the same time. She stated that she couldn't see her hand in front of her face, but she definitely could feel that she still had her full body and all of its five senses, memory, and full consciousness.

She described the enormous fear that was literally paralyzing her. She said, *"This is a fear that you have never felt in your life! I don't care what you may think, you have never felt fear until you are there in that place!"* The look on her face and the tone in her voice was intensely compelling.

But she continued on and stated how she suddenly saw a

If There's a Heaven, There Must Be a Hell

pinpoint of bright light in the distance that rushed towards her, and then instantly, she saw Jesus. "He just appeared right in front of me." She said that He never announced who He was; she just instantly knew it was Him. I asked her if she remembered what Jesus looked like; was His appearance like a bright light or spirit form? She replied, *"He didn't appear in that manner but He was in His earthly appearance like He was depicted in biblical movies or pictures except that I couldn't make the face out clearly, meaning He wasn't black, white, or Mexican."* Additionally, she added, *"I didn't care how He looked because I was more concerned about what He said!"*

I asked, "What did Jesus say?

She replied, *"He said, **'I told you that if you make your bed in Hell, that I would be there!'"*** Then she said, *"And I believe it because, honey, I was in Hell and He was there. He told me that if I didn't get my life together, then this is where I would end up!"* She recalled that she didn't know this scripture while she was living, but in that spiritual realm, she knew it immediately once Jesus spoke it to her as if she had known it all of her earthly life.

This was a staggering moment for me because, during my tutelage of learning about life and death, I had been grappling about this scripture in **Psalms 139:8: "If I ascend into heaven, You are there; If I make my bed in hell, behold, You are there" (NKJV).** God is so marvelous that He answered this burning question by providing a real-life experience to showcase the truth of this scripture. It was not ambiguous as I had believed it to be. But not only did He do that for me, but He also did it for her as well because that's the kind of God we serve!

For whatever reason, she had a burning question about Moses, if he went to be with the Lord since he didn't get to possess the

Promised Land because he disobeyed God. She went to her pastor, who was unable to answer her questions about what happened to Moses after God buried his body. I was able to provide her the answer; he did make it to be with the Lord, and God revealed it to us in Luke 9:28-31; however, as we venture out into the deep waters about Heaven and Sheol, we will learn that Moses did go to Heaven but not the Heaven that we think of today, which didn't occur for most of the Old Testaments Saints until after the resurrection of Jesus. In fact, they went to a part of Sheol, as we will examine. But for now, let's examine the scripture that answered her question. **Luke 9:28-31:**

"About eight days after Jesus said this, he took Peter, John and James with him and went up onto a mountain to pray. As he was praying, the appearance of his face changed, and his clothes became as bright as a flash of lightning. Two men, Moses and Elijah, appeared in glorious splendor, talking with Jesus. They spoke about his departure, which he was about to bring to fulfillment at Jerusalem. Peter and his companions were very sleepy, but when they became fully awake, they saw his glory and the two men standing with him. As the men were leaving Jesus, Peter said to him, 'Master, it is good for us to be here. Let us put up three shelters—one for you, one for Moses and one for Elijah.'"

She was absolutely enraptured to have this answer to her question!

She continued the recollection of her encounter. She recalled that when she came back into her body and opened her eyes, she wasn't worried about her son or any family. She just wanted to tell someone where she had been and to get her a Bible. This seems the most common recurring sentiment of NDE experiencers who have

If There's a Heaven, There Must Be a Hell

had this type of encounter. She is overjoyed to be serving the Lord now with a second chance at life. Glory to God!

Another personal account comes to mind as well, a patient that I will call Mitch. Mitch states that he was so dead that he already had a toe tag on his body. I said to Mitch, "See, that's why I don't know why they call it a near-death experience because you are dead!" He laughed and said, "Yes, I was toe tag dead about to be taken to the morgue. There was nothing near about it." Now Mitch described his account; he felt it was in a deep, black, dark, volcano-like area. He was hanging off the cliff for dear life, trying not to lose his grip because he could see a lake of fire and the flames down below him. He stated that he could hear people screaming and crying. He said that he asked God, "What have I done so bad that you would throw me in Hell?"

I asked him, "Did He answer you?"

He replied, "I heard His voice behind me, and I turned to look and there He was sitting on a rock in the middle of the flames, and He said, 'I've been waiting for you to call out to me!' I recall getting goosebumps from head to toe at that moment.

Mitch continued. "He saved my soul right there, and He told me that I have to go where He tells me and say to people whatever He tells me." There was a time when I would have found this too difficult to believe due to the inability to wrap my religious mind around this aspect of the unambiguous scripture that told us that if we make our beds in Hell, He will be there.

Another example of Jesus' display of everlasting mercy through an NDE was a young lady who died of a heroin overdose at a party. He allowed her spirit to go to Paradise and meet Jesus. She described how the angels were singing over her while waving their hands over her body and healing her mind and soul. She was also unknowingly pregnant. She had lost her husband and custody of her two daughters due to drug addiction. Her unborn baby was completely healthy despite her physical death.

The most remarkable cases that I ran across were featured on the TV show called *Project Afterlife* on *Destination America,* where a team of researchers from different professions interviews various people who have reported an NDE. A Navajo Native American man, who had died from a meth overdose, was dead for four hours while his wife sat over his body and prayed. I mention his ethnicity only to draw the point that he stated that culturally speaking, it was almost forbidden to talk about death. She explained how she was about to get emergency assistance, but she heard an audible voice that told her to "Stop, calm down, and pray." She closed the door and went and sat by her dead husband and prayed. Unknown to her, Jesus was doing a remarkable spiritual transformation of her husband on the other side in the spirit realm. Jesus took him to the ledge of Hell, where he could see the lake of fire. Also, Jesus took him to an empty pit in hell, which was actually dug for him. Jesus touched his shoulder and told him to listen, and he heard the prayers of his wife. Jesus told him that He was giving him a second chance, but it was only because of the faith and prayers of his wife. The man describes that Jesus literally took out his black, cold heart and replaced it with a clean new heart. I believe this to be both naturally and spiritually speaking. I know as a nurse that prolonged drug abuse will destroy the heart. In fact, he describes symptoms of what sounded like a massive heart attack from an overdose of methamphetamines. But isn't this the exact scriptural basis for **Ezekiel 36:26**: *"Moreover I will give you a new heart. I will put a new spirit within you. I will remove the stony heart from your flesh and give you a heart of flesh."* He had a visible surgical scar on his chest that his wife saw, and the man said that he had a soreness or muscle ache in his chest area as if he had surgery on his chest. He had a literal supernatural and physical open-heart transplant!

Another gentleman had a head-on collision after drinking and doing drugs and then driving after a party that resulted in him falling asleep at the wheel. He didn't see hell, but his spirit stayed in the hospital, and he found himself standing and watching his mother in the chapel at the hospital praying. He said that he was trying to tell her that he was there, but she couldn't see him. His mother confirmed that she could feel a spirit present about three different times, but she couldn't see anything. He stated that she was looking in the direction where he was standing by her side, but she couldn't hear him talking to her. Then a voice said to him that he needed to do what his mother was doing, and he lifted up his hands and yelled, "Jesus, if you are real, save me!" He said that, immediately, an enormous hand that felt about the size of the whole chapel rested on his head, and he tried to turn his head to look at who it was behind him, but he wasn't allowed to see Him. But the voice said that He was giving him another chance. The man was born again AFTER he died physically. I know Mormons and Catholics have their own practices for praying for the dead, but that's very different from this point of praying for someone right at the point of transitioning into death.

Religion would dictate to us that they should all have gone straight to Hell, correct? I had a patient who was literally in torment because her church group told her that her grandson went to hell because he died of a drug overdose and forbade her from having his funeral at the church. I watched her cry as she recounted how she knew he loved the Lord and was saved, but most of all, the prayer that he prayed with her the evening that he died had revealed his love for God. She stated, "That prayer was from a heart that loved God. It was so beautiful. I wish that you could have heard it. So, how could he be in hell?" My heart broke for her as I sat there comforting her. A sobering quote from Mahatma Gandhi says, *"Jesus is ideal and wonderful, but you Christians- you are not like him."* Wow! That should stab right in the heart any of us who claim the title of Christianity!

I am also reminded about the story of Ian McCormack, an atheist in the 1980s who died after being stung by a group of box jellyfish. He had a vision in the ambulance of his mother telling him that if he called on the name of the Lord, He would hear him and speak to him. However, he managed to get the broken words of the Lord's prayer, that he learned as a child, deep out of his spirit while on the brink of death riding in the ambulance. He died while in the emergency department at the hospital. He ended up having an incredible experience in Heaven but was given a choice to stay or go back. What caused him to come back was the thought of his mother and how she would be grieved for the rest of her life because she would have thought that he was spending the rest of his existence in hell. She did not know that while in the clutch of death's jowls, he had a vision of her praying and telling him to cry out to God, and he did!

I boldly proclaim to anyone—do NOT judge where you think someone is or is not spending eternity. I have seen first-hand the type of spiritual encounter that the Lord can have with someone even though they have technically crossed from life to death. God knew that I would be overly grieved with thoughts that my son would spend all eternity in Hell. Therefore, He allowed me to see into the heavenlies what transpired in my son's real-life of his eternal soul and spirit at the time of his death. Seeing this miraculous spiritual exchange between Jesus and my son, I can make a definitive statement that you cannot imagine the enormousness of love and mercy of the Lord! In writing this, my heart wells up all over again with the feelings of the unconditional love of Christ that was present in Paradise. I am sincerely anticipating sharing the full details of this account with you. The day that I got the news of my son's death that night, the Holy Spirit kept saying, "He chose to stay." It seems that I heard that a million times, but I didn't know what that meant. "Who, how, where, what...does that mean?" I was so perplexed by those words, while feeling like I was in a bad dream. Of course, this was days before my encounter with the Lord that would reveal what those words meant. I didn't know that He was on the cusp of bringing the answers to my perplexity in trying to decipher, "How could he choose anything if he was dead?"

I am not going to get into any theological and religious debates of "Once saved, always saved" or "deathbed confessions," etc. Jesus is so simple; religion is not! But I know that just as Jude stated, some are going to be saved by snatching them out of the fire. **"Keep yourselves in the love of God, eagerly waiting for the mercy of our Lord Yeshua the Messiah that leads to eternal life. And have mercy on those who are wavering— save them by snatching them out of the fire" Jude 1:21-23.** Why would the Lord instruct us to have mercy upon others who are struggling and save them with such passion like snatching them out of the fire but then Himself not operate with the same mercy? Again, I will state that He is not schizophrenic, bipolar, or hypocritical, as many of us are. Oh, we have no idea of how grandiose His love and mercy. I saw it, and I felt it; His whole being is mercy! He doesn't just grant it; He literally is it! Hallelujah!

I am not coming from a place of universalism theology that says EVERYBODY goes to heaven. I do not believe that. I know Hell is real and I know there will be people who are there and many who will go there. Not everyone is going to accept Christ as Lord and Savior. But for those who have, His longsuffering and mercy are more powerful than our shortcomings and failures that religion would deem worthy of death. I've seen it first-hand, as we will get to later. But for now, the account of Jesus with the woman that was caught in the act of adultery in **John 8**, is a perfect montage of our compassionate, yet Holy Savior.

The religious men were there with their stones in their hands, ready to condemn and kill her for being caught in the act of adultery. But the Compassionate One knelt down and began to write on the ground. We don't know what He wrote because the Bible does not say. But what if He began to write down every one of those men's unrepented sins (i.e., Paul - stealing, James- lying, Michael - pride, Richard - envy)? In His compassion, He didn't permit them to stone the woman and kill her, thus allowing her to die in her sin. So, He did this:

"'Teacher, this woman was caught in the act of adultery. In the Law Moses commanded us to stone such women. Now what do you say?' They were using this question as a trap, in order to have a basis for accusing him. But Jesus bent down and started to write on the ground with his finger. When they kept on questioning him, he straightened up and said to them, 'Let any one of you who is without sin be the first to throw a stone at her.' Again, He stooped down and wrote on the ground. At this, those who heard began to go away one at a time, the older ones first, until only Jesus was left, with the woman still standing there. Jesus straightened up and asked her, 'Woman, where are

they? Has no one condemned you?' 'No one, sir,' she said. 'Then neither do I condemn you,' Jesus declared. 'Go now and leave your life of sin.'"

Christ was the only man standing that could have easily condemned her because He was perfect and without sin; therefore, according to the Law, He could have proceeded to stone her. Yet, He did not! He was revealing to them the same spiritual principle that was spoken in **James 2:10-11 (NIV):** *"Whoever keeps the whole law but stumbles at just one point is guilty of breaking all of it. For He who said, 'Do not commit adultery,' also said, 'Do not murder.' If you do not commit adultery, but do commit murder, you have become a lawbreaker."* The religious leaders were ready to commit murder in addition to what other hidden sins caused them to drop their stones one by one. They may or may not have been guilty of adultery, so they remained righteous in their own eyes. Isn't this precisely what Jesus referred to as worrying about the speck in your brother or sister's eye while having a beam in your own? *"Stop judging, so that you may not be judged. For with the judgment you judge, you will be judged; and with the measure you use, it will be measured to you. Why do you look at the speck in your brother's eye, but do not notice the beam in your own eye?" Matthew 7:1-3.*

Moreover, Christ didn't ask if they were guilty of the SAME sin, just sin. As they reflected on their own lives, the rocks fell out of their hands one by one. He didn't come to condemn us but save us and give us eternal life.

"If you do not believe the earthly things I told you, how will you believe when I tell you about heavenly things? No one has gone up into heaven except the One who came down from heaven—the Son of Man. Just as Moses lifted up the serpent in

the desert, so the Son of Man must be lifted up, so that whoever believes in Him may have eternal life! For God so loved the world that He gave His one and only Son, that whoever believes in Him shall not perish but have eternal life. God did not send the Son into the world to condemn the world, but in order that the world might be saved through Him. The one who believes in Him is not condemned; but whoever does not believe has been condemned already, because he has not put his trust in the name of the one and only Ben-Elohim" John 3:12-18.

Yet, it's important to address that Christ didn't give her a free pass to keep living in sin, for He is holy. He said, "Go now and leave your life of sin." Leaving and turning away from the things that are not pleasing to God is repentance. But even in our struggles, there is NOTHING that can separate us from the love and pursuit of God. He still leaves the 99 to go after one of His lost sheep. *"Now all the tax collectors and sinners were drawing near to hear Yeshua. The Pharisees and the Torah scholars began to complain, saying, 'This man welcomes sinners and eats with them.' So He told this parable to them, saying, 'Which man among you, if he has a hundred sheep and loses one of them, will not leave the ninety-nine in the wilderness and go after the lost one until he finds it? When he has found it, he puts it on his shoulders, rejoicing. And when he comes home, he calls together his friends and neighbors and says, 'Rejoice with me, for I've found my sheep that was lost!' I tell you, in the same way there will be more joy in heaven over one repenting sinner than over the ninety-nine righteous people who have no need of repentance. Or which woman, if she has ten silver coins and loses one coin, does not light a lamp, sweep the house, and search thoroughly until she finds it? When she has found it, she calls together her friends and neighbors, saying, 'Rejoice with me, for I've found the coin I had lost!' In the same way, I tell you, there is joy in the presence of the angels of God over one sinner who repents" Luke 15:1-10.* This was Jesus talking to the stiff-necked, prideful, self-righteous religious men of that day, in whom He was in direct opposition with. As we see, He will go after that lost sheep, even to the depths of hell.

We must have a heart that strives to live righteously. He gives us chances beyond what we deserve because of His grace and mercy, just as He did for the adulterous woman. So, if He had compassion for this woman's brokenness and struggles, He will have that same compassion for ours, also. We should be willing to obey His correction and guidance through His word. Yeshua knew that He was the living water that could satisfy the longing in her soul. We have the living water of the Holy Spirit to empower us, which was way more than what she had at that time. She only had the Law of Moses, which was meant to give some governance to man's sinful nature, but it was futile in changing men's hearts. But the Mediator was right there with her to forgive her sin. He didn't tell her to go sacrifice a bull or lamb. He had not died yet physically, but His purpose as the spotless lamb that would take away the sins of the world had already been fulfilled. He is the beginning and the end.

Satan's most prominent stratagem is to blind the hearts and minds of men to the love and compassion of the loving Heavenly Father. The beautiful biblical narrative in **Psalms 103:8-14 (NIV)** is picturesque of a loving Father God and not the God painted in the Sistine Chapel.

"The Lord is compassionate and gracious, slow to anger, abounding in love. He will not always accuse, nor will He harbor His anger forever; He does not treat us as our sins deserve or repay us according to our iniquities. For as high as

the heavens are above the earth, so great is His love for those who fear him; as far as the east is from the west, so far has he removed our transgressions from us. As a father has compassion on His children, so the Lord has compassion on those who fear Him; for He knows how we are formed, He remembers that we are dust." The Hebrew word for fear is **yare,** which means *morally reverent.* He doesn't want us to be afraid of Him but desires a reverence towards Him. Does this scriptural narrative describe an angry, quick-tempered God who is full of wrath and ready to throw us into Hell? We are His portion, the apple of His eye. He knows us down to the very number of hairs that we have on our heads. If you are bald, He knows the number of hair follicles that He placed there (Luke 12:7). He is the Great Physician that came for the sick, which is the loss sinner. *"I did not come to call the [self-proclaimed] righteous [who see no need to repent], but sinners to repentance [to change their old way of thinking, to turn from sin and to seek God and His righteousness]"* Luke 5:32 (AMP).

If God is all-knowing, then He knew that man would disobey Him and eat of the Tree of Knowledge, correct? However, He still chose to create a living soul made in His image to have fellowship with. We are His splendor. David's Psalm illustrates in **Chapter 8:4-7** just how much the creation of man means to Him: *"When I consider Your heavens, the work of Your fingers, the moon and the stars, which You established—what is man, that You are mindful of him? And the son of man, that You care for him? Yet You made him a little lower than the angels, and crowned him with glory and majesty! You gave him dominion over the works of Your hands. You put all things under their feet."* This reflects His mindfulness for us, and He will always be, even if or when ours is not on Him. This is what has set Satan against God's creation, and we need to understand that he is not bound up in Hell just yet. So, who is this entity named Satan? Let's discover the answer in the next chapter.

Allow God to soften your heart and work in your life to accept the truth of His finished work on the cross. I'm not going to write some scripted prayer for you to say, as I have seen in other books, and that's perfectly fine for authors who wish to do that. But my heart reflects the desire of the Father, Son, and Holy Spirit who desires for us to have a personal conversation with Him. Take a lesson from that thief on the cross. If you call out to the Lord, He will hear you and answer. ***"Adonai is righteous in all His ways and kind in all His deeds. Adonai (God) is near to all who call on Him, to all who call on Him in truth. He will fulfill the desire of those who fear (reverent respect) Him. He will hear their cry and save them" Psalm 145:17-19.***

My salvation experience is still very vivid for me. Spirituality has been the foundation of my life since the young age of ten years old. In 1979, my childhood church was a traditional African American Baptist church that preached sermons that were, at best, good Bible stories that directed you to the concept of a larger higher power that existed beyond ourselves. Yet, we didn't use the words or salvation concepts that I have come to know today, such as "getting born-again," "saved," and "turning your life over to the Lord." But somehow, the act of joining the church and getting baptized was synonymous with getting saved.

But one significant Sunday morning, for the first time in my young life, I felt something so real and tangible, like an influx of warm olive oil was poured out and flowed throughout my soul. The immeasurable presence of unconditional love and acceptance permeated all through me, the real me, the broken and burdened child who was living in unimaginable brokenness in my home. I felt hopeless, fearful, and scorned by the mental and emotional conditions of our home life. Sitting and reflecting on the despair, my hot face began to flood with salty tears as they sang:

"Because He lives, I can face tomorrow. Because He lives, all fear is gone. And because I know oh oh who holds my future. My life is worth the living just because He lives."

As if The Father God stooped down and spoke those words directly to me, my spirit was endowed with hope and love, like a warm blanket coming down from Heaven and wrapping me in it. In a blink of an eye, I knew that life was still worth living because HE LIVES! I felt I could survive this dysfunctional home because HE LIVES! In one momentous splendor of supernatural spiritual awakening, I gained the full spiritual understanding of who this big unknown God of the Bible stories whom I heard about Sunday after Sunday, and HE LIVES! But miraculously, I felt the majestic Savior touch me with His divine hand and calmed that crushed, depressed soul, and I knew He was now with me. He birthed in my spirit the sense that He knew me before He ever placed me in my mother's womb (Jeremiah 1:5); although I didn't have the knowledge of this scripture at that time, I had the experience of it. He was personal to me, and I accepted all that He was, is, and is to come! I'm sure the onlooking congregation had no idea what was really taking place in this little girl. Even at 50 years old, that experience remains very vivid and so emotional that I tear up when I reflect on it. I didn't have a scripted "Sinners Prayer," and I didn't need it. I was the thief on the cross that was simply crying out, "Lord, remember me." Accepting Christ and having our old sinful hearts renewed and reborn into the truth of The Savior is the most miraculous spiritual encounter that anyone can have.

God the Father was no longer the far away, unattainable hero that was the mastermind behind Daniel and the lions' den, or Noah and the Ark. But He was now my Hero. In the innocence of youth, who didn't yet know there was also a hero of evil named the devil that influenced the actions of men. I say this to let you know that accepting Jesus doesn't make all earthly problems go away, but it does help you deal with them with the strength and power of the Holy Spirit.

He is a personal God, and the Friend and person of the Holy Spirit will come and abide with you. Jesus had to go away physically, but He said that He would not be leaving us alone, but the Holy Spirit would come and dwell with us. The Good News is summed up *in Romans 1:1-4: "For the Good News of God, which He announced beforehand through His prophets in the Holy Scriptures, concerning His Son, He came into being from the seed of David according to the flesh. He was appointed Ben-Elohim (Son of God) in power according to the Ruach of holiness by the resurrection from the dead. He is Messiah Yeshua (Jesus) our Lord."*

The narrow road that leads to eternal life is only traveled when we have accepted Jesus as Lord and Savior. Someone may be saying to themselves, "Well, I have never seen Him, so how can I believe in Him?" That is a very human reaction, and He understood the human logic personified to many of us by His disciple, Thomas. Theologians have commonly referred to him as "Doubting Thomas." But aren't you glad that The Messiah doesn't identify us by our weaknesses and failures? Instead, He knows the number of hairs on our heads, and our name is engraved in the palm of His hand. *"'Lord,' said Thomas, 'we do not know where You are going, so how can we know the way?' Jesus answered, 'I am the way, the truth, and the life. No one comes to the Father except through Me. If you had known Me, you would know My Father as well. From now on you do know Him and have seen Him'"* **John 14:5-7 (NIV).**

Jesus left him with a hallmark statement in **John 20:29**: *"Jesus said to him, 'Have you believed because you have seen me? Blessed are those who have not seen and yet have believed.'"* So, how much more blessed are those who have faith to believe without touching the nail prints and the wound in His side?

Romans 10:8-10 gives us the direction to understanding and receiving the plan of salvation that we should build upon to grow and live in Him. *"'The word is near you, in your mouth and in your heart'—that is, the word of faith that we are proclaiming:*

For if you confess with your mouth that Yeshua is Lord, and believe in your heart that God raised Him from the dead, you will be saved. For with the heart it is believed for righteousness, and with the mouth it is confessed for salvation."

If you have made this most vital decision today, all of Heaven is celebrating! Welcome home to the family.

Chapter 6

Satan, That Serpent of Ole and The Host of Fallen Angels

There are two great forces, God's force of good and the devil's force of evil, and I believe Satan is alive and he is working, and he is working harder than ever, and we have many mysteries that we don't understand. ~ Billy Graham

Satan's rage is against the inhabitants of the earth. Imagine as he was beholding this noblest creation that captured his eye and perplexed his mind: a being who was made in the image of God. The Holy Spirit revealed that Satan studied man and all of creation long before he found the resoluteness to attempt to deceive again. He had deceived one-third of the angelic host that he was in charge of to rebel with him before they were expelled from Heaven. Satan outwitted our father and mother of the earth, Adam and Chava (Eve). He coveted the position of God. Therefore, he coveted man's position with God and the dominion that was given to us! He hoped that sin and death would forever separate man and God.

Furthermore, according to **Revelation 12:12,** Satan knows that his time was limited from the time that he was expelled to earth, and in the grand scheme of eternity, his time is short. *"Therefore rejoice, O heavens, and you who dwell in them! Woe to the earth and the sea, for the devil has come down to you with great rage,* *knowing that his time is short."* Satan's main objective was to take our dominion from the place of his habitation, which is the earth.

Although Adam walked with God in the cool of the day, he failed to protect the character of God to his wife. All Satan ever has to do is promote doubt about what God has said or who He says that we are. We see this clearly in the account of the temptation of Jesus in the wilderness with Satan saying, "IF, you are the Son of God…" More than the overt temptation itself, such as turning the stone into bread, there was embedded the subtle temptation to make Jesus doubt who He was. Therefore, if we cannot trust Him and who He is, then we cannot fulfill the complete exhortation to worship Him in The Spirit and in The Truth. *"For The Spirit is God, and it is fitting that those who worship him worship in The Spirit and in The Truth"* **John 4:24 (ABPE).**

Satan lost his position and dominion in heaven, but he didn't lose his powers as a rebellious fallen chief angel whose new dominion became the earth. *1 Peter 5:8* gives a metaphor of how his roaming is like that of a lion. Satan is restless on this earth. He is not yet chained up in Hell as we might envision. In the book of Job, the Lord asked Satan where he had come from, and Satan responded, *"From roaming the earth and from walking on it" Job 1:7.* However, he is not roaming aimlessly about. His activity has purpose and intention.

We are starkly cautioned by these words: *"Stay alert! Watch out! Your adversary the devil prowls around like a roaring lion, searching for someone to devour" 1 Peter 5:8.* And know this, when he finds someone to devour, he looks to kill, steal, and destroy, according to **John 10:10.** But Christ said that He came so that we may have LIFE and life more abundantly. *"The devil's finest trick is to persuade you that he does not exist." Charles Baudelaire, Le Spleen de Paris.*

It would be millenniums before Christ would arrive on earth to be the ransom Lamb of God to take away the sins of the world and conquer death. In the meantime, it was a tumultuous time for man, who became exceedingly wicked. The Angels that were assigned as the watchers over the earth ended up being enticed by the beauty of human women and fell from their natural spiritual positions by having sex and marrying the women. This produced the Nephilim (giants) in the earth (***Genesis 6:1-8 TLV)***. This bears some similarity to Greek mythology, where the gods impregnated beautiful women and had powerful children that were half-gods and half-human.

"Now when humankind began to multiply on the face of the ground and daughters were born to them, then the sons of God saw that the daughters of men were good and they took for themselves wives, any they chose. Then Adonai said, 'My Spirit will not remain with humankind forever, since they are flesh. So their days will be 120 years. The Nephilim were on the earth in those days, and also afterward, whenever the sons of God came to the daughters of men, and gave birth to them. Those were the mighty men of old, men of renown.

"Then Adonai saw that the wickedness of humankind was great on the earth, and that every inclination of the thoughts of their heart was only evil all the time. So Adonai regretted that He made humankind on the earth, and His heart was deeply pained. So Adonai said, 'I will wipe out humankind, whom I have created, from the face of the ground, from humankind to livestock, crawling things and the flying creatures of the sky, because I regret that I made them.' But Noah found favor in Adonai's eyes."

I have read and studied the complete, fascinating **Book of Enoch,** which is one of the most important apocryphal works that was ever canonized in the King James's version of the Bible but was not included in the Vulgate, translated in Latin by Jerome of Stridon. Therefore, so many religions do not accept it as part of the Bible, although it was found with the famous Dead Sea Scrolls with the other canonized works that are a part of the KJV. It possesses great details and prophecy of the future and details the antiquity of man. In my Jewish Roots studies at my home church, we studied the church fathers like Justin Martyr and Clement of Alexandria, who referenced The Book of Enoch in many of their commentaries. This enabled me to be well-versed and confident in the material that I am presenting to you about this particular aspect of biblical history.

Enoch presents an extensive portrayal of Genesis' watcher angels who married earthly women. These were not part of the one-third of the Heavenly Host that rebelled and were cast out with Satan. These were 200 angels who committed the sin of defiling human nature by taking on human form to cohabitate with women. Enoch lists the archangels and the leaders' names. These angels were called The Watchers. Please read as follows:

"And it came to pass when the children of men had multiplied that in those days were born unto them beautiful and comely daughters. And the angels, the children of the heaven, saw and lusted after them, and said to one another: 'Come, let us choose us wives from among the children of men and beget us children.' And Semjaza, who was their leader, said unto them: 'I fear ye will not indeed agree to do this deed, and I alone shall have to pay the penalty of a great sin.' And they all answered him and said: 'Let us all swear an oath, and all bind ourselves by mutual imprecations not to abandon this plan but to do this thing.' Then sware they all together and bound themselves by mutual

imprecations upon it. And they were in all two hundred; who descended in the days of Jared on the summit of Mount Hermon, and they called it Mount Hermon, because they had sworn and bound themselves by mutual imprecations upon it. And these are the names of their leaders: Sêmîazâz, their leader, Arâkîba, Râmêêl, Kôkabîêl, Tâmîêl, Râmîêl, Dânêl, Êzêqêêl, Barâqîjâl, Asâêl, Armârôs, Batârêl, Anânêl, Zaqîêl, Samsâpêêl, Satarêl, Tûrêl, Jômjâêl, Sariêl. These are their chiefs of tens.

"And all the others together with them took unto themselves wives, and each chose for himself one, and they began to go in unto them and to defile themselves with them, and they taught them charms and enchantments, and the cutting of roots, and made them acquainted with plants. And they became pregnant, and they bare great giants, whose height was three thousand ells: Who consumed all the acquisitions of men. And when men could no longer sustain them, the giants turned against them and devoured mankind. And they began to sin against birds, and beasts, and reptiles, and fish, and to devour one another's flesh, and drink the blood. Then the earth laid accusation against the lawless ones" Enoch Chapters 6 and 7.

This exceedingly wicked mixed race of human and angelic beings caused God to regret making man. **"For God did not spare angels when they sinned, but threw them into Sheol. He put them in chains of gloomy darkness, to be held until the judgment. He did not spare the ancient world. He preserved only Noah, a proclaimer of righteousness, along with seven others, when He brought a flood upon the world of the ungodly. He devastated the cities of Sodom and Gomorrah, reducing them to ashes—making them an example of what is going to happen to the ungodly"** 2 Peter 2:4-6.

Enoch further details what occurred with all of the evil participants of the downfall of the human race, the angels, women, and by-product mixed species of angelic and human, in the following Enoch Chapter 15. We know that Satan came to kill, steal, and destroy. He is not alone in the spirit realm; he has much help. After the flood, the disembodied Nephilim remained on the earth as demons. The angels are chained in Sheol until the final judgment.

Satan set in his heart and mind to ascend his throne above God and Heaven. He wasn't content to think of himself as equal with God. He wanted to be above and higher than God's authority. He was equipped with powers and beauty and took authority over one-third of the angelic host. He was one of the cherubs that covered the throne of God. Satan's spiritual being abides on earth and rules through principalities and powers of darkness in the air. **Ephesians 2:2** declares: *"At that time, you walked in the way of this world, in conformity to the ruler of the domain of the air—the ruler of the spirit who is now operating in the sons of disobedience"*

God gave a stunning and masterful account of what happened to the angels and their offspring: *"But you were formerly spiritual, living the eternal life, and immortal for all generations of the world. And therefore I have not appointed wives for you; for as for the spiritual ones of the heaven, in heaven is their dwelling. And now, the giants, who are produced from the spirits and flesh, shall be called evil spirits upon the earth, and on the earth shall be their dwelling. Evil spirits have proceeded from their bodies; because they are born from men, and from the holy Watchers is their beginning and primal origin; they shall be evil spirits on earth, and evil spirits shall they be called. As for the spirits of heaven, in heaven shall be their dwelling, but as for the spirits of the earth which were born upon the earth, on the earth shall be their dwelling. And the spirits of the giants afflict, oppress, destroy, attack, do battle, and work destruction on the earth, and cause trouble: they take no food, but nevertheless hunger and thirst, and cause offences. And these spirits shall rise up against the children of men and against the women, because they have proceeded from them."* This is what we call demons, but now we understand their origins and how they assimilated upon the earth.

BUT, Jesus remembered and mediated for Noah and his family, the only righteous left upon the earth. You may wonder why I said that Jesus remembered, so allow me to explain.

I Timothy 2:5-6 states this with simple clarity. *"For there is one God and there is one Mediator between God and men—a human, Messiah Yeshua, who gave Himself as a ransom for all—the testimony at the proper time".* Jesus has been and will always be our Mediator. **Romans 8:34** says: *"It is Messiah, who died, and moreover was raised, and is now at the right hand of God and who also intercedes for us".*

When the flood came to destroy all flesh on the earth, the spirits of the giants became disembodied from the flesh, but their spirits did not cease to exist, just as our spirit will continue to exist after we die. Therefore, they were released upon the earth and wreaked havoc on mankind. They desire to take us captive and destroy us. But thanks be to God, who always causes us to triumph through Christ Jesus!

Therefore, if we don't believe that Satan and demons exist and exist with a purpose, then we will blame all the good and all the bad on God or choose not to believe in God at all. *"If there is a loving God, then why is there so much bad in the world?"* or *"Why do bad things happen to good people?"* Does this sound familiar? But we fail to give credit where credit is due. We have an adversary who inhabits the earth and has an agenda. **John 10:10-*11*: *"The thief comes only to steal, slaughter, and destroy. I have come that they might have life, and have it abundantly! "I am the Good Shepherd. The Good Shepherd lays down His life for the sheep."***

Our biggest adversary that Satan devoured with was when he brought physical death to earth's realm. So, let's get honest.

Chapter 7

It's Time to Get Honest

"Honesty is of God and dishonesty of the devil; the devil was a liar from the beginning" ~ Joseph B Wirthlin

To shift our mindset about death, we must identify the REAL culprit of this dark plague of life. The Church should be well-versed in how to biblically deal with death because it is the most spiritual experience second to being born-again. Yet, our attempts to spiritualize it clearly fall short with using clichés like: "the Lord giveth and the Lord taketh away," "God just needed him/her more than you," or "Heaven has gained another angel." Let me add, we do not turn into angels after we die. There is no scriptural basis for this cliché. None of these clichés produce any comfort to the hurting, bereaved heart. Better yet, it is emotionally schizophrenic to go for comfort to the God that we credit as the culprit that has caused the very pain you need comfort from.

God ALWAYS gets the blame for death regardless of the circumstances. The Lord gives, but He doesn't take away. Satan has hidden and camouflaged himself behind the name of God to bring offense against Him for death on the earth. However, in the Book of Hebrews, it overtly defines who had power over death. But Jesus defeated the power of death by restoring eternal life; however, the occurrence of physical death could not be undone. When He told

Adam that he would surely die if he ate from the Tree, He knew the wages of sin would be death, and He cannot lie. God had to watch man make a choice to die physically and spiritually, yet He didn't intervene in man's free will to choose. He gave us free will out of a relationship, not a dictatorship. He was and is still mindful of us. But in the meantime, while physical death isn't yet released from the earth, death can never be experienced again once in Paradise. Death will remain on the earth until this earth is done away with, and The New Earth and New Heaven are established at the second coming of Christ. ***"Then I saw a new heaven and a new earth; for the first heaven and the first earth had passed away, and the sea was no more" Revelation 21:1.*** He came the first time as a baby, but this time He will return as the Reigning King. Hallelujah!

Satan thought that his deception would break the bonds of fellowship and eternal life in Eden between man and the divine Trinity of God by causing man to die. Envision Satan's jealousy that boiled like hot lava as he saw Adam and the Lord fellowshipping together, in the cool of the day. Can you imagine Satan's fury as he looked intently at this enigma of the one and only creation made in the image of God? After all, just like himself, all of the angels have been created but not fashioned in God's likeness. He coveted man's worship of the Creator. He still hates our fellowship with God. He lost the war in heaven; now, this created being has been placed into a perfect created domain on earth. **Revelation 12:7-12 (NIV):** ***"And war broke out in heaven: Michael and his angels fought with the dragon; and the dragon and his angels fought, but they did not prevail, nor was a place found for them in heaven any longer. So the great dragon was cast out—that serpent of old, called the Devil and Satan, who deceives the whole world; he was cast to the earth, and his angels were cast out with him."***

I can hear him say in his heart, "I heard Elohim say that if Adam ate of the Tree of Knowledge, he would surely die. So that's it! I must cause them to eat the fruit so that all can be destroyed through death." Not only would man die, but the perfected vegetation and fruitfulness of Eden, plus the animals, would as well.

The Holy Spirit revealed that Satan studied man long before he found the resoluteness to attempt to deceive man into rebellion against God. He is the master manipulator, as seen from his history of deceiving one-third of the angelic host of Heaven. Satan vainly imagined that he could defeat God, just as he vainly accused Job of worshipping God only because of the wealth and goodness in Job's life. Satan was and will continue to be our accuser. *"And the great dragon was thrown down—the ancient serpent, called the devil and satan, who deceives the whole world. He was thrown down to the earth, and his angels were thrown down with him. Then I heard a loud voice in heaven saying, "Now have come the salvation and the power and the kingdom of our God and the authority of His Anointed One, for the accuser of our brothers and sisters—the one who accuses them before our God day and night—has been thrown out" Revelation 12:9-10*. The Lord had already charged Satan that he could take anything of Job's, but not his life. Satan is so callous as the ruler of death that he chose to kill all of Job's children at one time. Therefore, it is plausible to imagine how easy it was for Job to credit God for these acts because a spiritual enemy wasn't identified as the culprit of misdeeds during this ancient era.

Job was not any different than most of us today. I never blamed God for my son's death. Nonetheless, in the depths of my sorrow and despair, I initially felt that my prayers for protection to keep my son from all hurt, harm, or danger had not been answered.

After All, I had been praying and confessing over my family, "you shall live and not die and declare the works of the Lord." As I am thrust into unbridled honesty with myself, similar to Job's prayers every day on behalf of his children in case they sinned, were our prayers as parents commenced out of fear and anxiety rather than faith? ***Job 3:25*** discloses his greatest fear, and I uttered the same sentiment when I lost my child: ***"What I feared has come upon me; what I dreaded has happened to me."*** Like any parent, the biggest fear and dread above all else is the anxiety and despair that comes with the mere thought of having to bury a child.

Exceptionally speaking, however, the Holy Spirit profoundly revealed that the Psalmist's declaration of ***"I shall not die but live and declare the works of the Lord" (Psalm 118:17)*** is not negated by physical life and death. Meaning, that even when we die physically, we still live to declare the works of the Lord as we honor and praise Him for all eternity in our heavenly home. The souls in Heaven constantly speak of the works, glory, and goodness of the Lord. Just as some people do not get healed on this side of life but are healed and whole in their life-after-life. There are all sorts of physical and mental infirmities that did not get healed on this side of life, but most certainly are in the glorified body. Thus, we shall live and not die!

Seneca Sodi had an experience in the early 1900s where he went to Heaven for 40 days. He spoke about the feeling of freedom being released from his physical body. Also, there was a lady that he knew on earth that had been handicapped and bound to a wheelchair. He saw her and realized who it was, but her body was whole and healed without the need for her wheelchair. She was overjoyed to be released from her suffering and was now bathed in the light of abounding love and overwhelming joy.

This is our hope for any loved one who accepted their Savior but left this life with a body riddled from the ravages of cancer, AIDS, dementia, rheumatoid arthritis, and all other manners of illness and tragedies like decapitation, burned bodies, etc. We couldn't have dreamed of a better God!

God does not use the death of a loved one as punishment. Yet, we often interpret it this manner because we believe that God is powerful enough to stop anything. And He is. However, when He doesn't stop what we think He should, particularly death, then we become angry, confused, or worse yet, we doubt His love and goodness. This is Satan's finest assault on our minds. If he can get us to question the goodness and love of God, then the rest of the attacks against God is like taking candy from a baby. But we should learn from Job that God doesn't cut us a deal under the table based on our assumptions of our good behavior or great works for Him. Falsely believing that we will not have to endure anything too burdensome or sorrowful to suffer through, merely because we are "Christians," will cause great spiritual misunderstandings about our relationship with The Creator.

In essence, we allude that we have some sort of preferential treatment from Him to withhold any manner of suffering, especially this inevitable most natural part of life. But if this was the case, the apostles who established the Church would have escaped suffering and death. On the contrary, we know they were not only warned by Christ Himself that they would suffer, but they embraced it.

But in our modern Christendom and other religious views, this is where we silently (so we think) accuse God in our hearts for our loved one's passing away, and we spiritualize our thoughts by uttering, "The Lord gives, and He takes away" or "Though He may slay me, yet will I trust Him." Job expresses himself in multiple dialogues with himself, his friends, and his wife. Here lies the quandary of quoting these scriptures: They are partly quoted, thus missing the true golden nuggets that God wants us to invest in our spirits.

What if God does slay and take away, will you answer as Job did? *Job 13:15: "Even if He slays me, I will wait for Him."* Job authorized his soul to wait for the vindication of the Lord amid pain and suffering. *Job 1:21-22: "Then Job got up, tore his robe, shaved his head, fell to the ground and worshiped. Then he said: 'Naked I came from my mother's womb, and naked I will return there. Adonai gave and Adonai has taken away; blessed be the Name of Adonai.' Through all this, Job did not sin nor did he cast reproach on God."*

Wow! Do you grasp this? Although Job made these statements erroneously as acts by God, he didn't hold an ill charge against Him. But the truth that we need to unpack is that it was Satan who was stealing, killing, and destroying, NOT GOD! God charged Satan that he could not take Job's life. The Lord gave, but Satan took away. This is where we have misunderstood the dictates of Job's narrative. Most noteworthy, God didn't kill Job's children or inflict his body with boils, but Job accepted this as God's hand, but his poignant words are so powerful. *"'Should we accept the good from God and not accept the bad?' Through all this Job did not sin with his lips" (Job 2:10).*

Nonetheless, although Job credited God for the affliction, he reverenced and honored Him in the good and the bad! That is magnificent in and of itself, much like how we will thank God for the sun but then curse Him for the thunderstorm or tornado. I have recounted numerous people who spoke of their decision to stop believing in or walking with God because of a tragedy or death that has occurred in their lives. If we could allow the Holy Spirit to teach us how to lay hold to Job's unwavering commitment to stay anchored to God, whether blessed or in lack, whether during good or bad, whether in life or death, then we would have mastered real faith.

However, Job was unaware that it was Satan who was brutally attacking his family, possessions, health, and mind. It is crucial to understand the ancient Hebrew mindset of being a monotheistic belief system. Although they were separate people that believed in one God while surrounded by many nations who worshiped false gods and idols, there was not much, if any, understanding of an evil spiritual entity who opposed God and His creation. They were well acquainted with human enemies that opposed them and seemingly were at war with these enemies during most of the Old Testament. There are few accounts in the OT that speak of Satan being an adversary, such as Job and Zechariah.

Moreover, Genesis, which is the beginning, first gives a glimpse of Satan's character through the serpent who beguiled Eve. However, it's not until the story continues in the Gospels that we truly see the full manifestation of Satan as he arrives back on to the scene and tries to tempt Jesus in the wilderness after He had fasted 40 days and nights. Moreover, the rest of the NT is full of a plethora of scriptures and accounts of him as an evil spiritual entity.

Therefore, through scripture, we are now able to be well-versed in who Satan is, but Job did not have this knowledge and understanding. Nonetheless, although we have access to these scriptures, a large portion of our modern culture demonstrates a similar lack of knowledge and understanding. Job credited God for giving and taking away; likewise, we profess the same rhetoric. There's no excuse for this misconception. God left us the manual to defeat the work of Satan. Jesus came to earth to defeat the works of

Satan, and that includes death *"because the devil has been sinning from the beginning. The reason the Son of God appeared was to destroy the devil's work" (I John 3:8).*

The Church has used the Book of Job to glorify suffering, especially during funerals and eulogies. Consequently, we have missed the rich, spiritually maturing premise. Can we worship and honor God even in grief and suffering? *"And after you have suffered a little while, the God of all grace, who has called you to his eternal glory in Christ, will himself restore, confirm, strengthen, and establish you" I Peter 5:10 (ESV).* Isn't this precisely what occurred in Job's life? Most people will never endure Job's magnitude of calamity. However, when we are suffering, especially grief, it is just as profoundly painful. But let's allow ourselves to glorify Job's ability to avoid cursing God as Satan had predicted that he would. The more Job stood, the more defiant Satan became in his attacks to destroy him. Job had some pity parties and cursed the day he was born but refrained from cursing God and upheld Him in worship in word and deed. I find it alluring how he viewed death. Let's take a sidestep and read his words regarding how much better death is versus the suffering of this life. This was during his despair as he cursed the day he was born. *"Why did I not perish at birth, and die as I came from the womb? Why were there knees to receive me and breasts that I might be nursed? For now I would be lying down in peace; I would be asleep and at rest with kings and rulers of the earth, who built for themselves places now lying in ruins, with princes who had gold, who filled their houses with silver. Or why was I not hidden away in the ground like a stillborn child, like an infant who never saw the light of day? There the wicked cease from turmoil, and there the weary are at rest. Captives also enjoy their ease; they no longer hear the slave driver's shout. The small and the great are there, and the slaves are freed from their owners. Why is light given to those in misery, and life to the bitter of soul, to those who long for death that does not come, who search for it more than for hidden treasure, who are filled with gladness and rejoice when they reach the grave? Why is life given to a man whose way is hidden?" (Job 3:11-23).*

Job was riveted by the thought of death being a much better state and condition than living in a world of suffering and pain. We often reference a loved one as "being in a better place." Do we sincerely believe this? Or is it a cliché that sounds good and tickles the ears? If we do believe it, do we believe it with as equal fervor as Job? Are we persuaded that our loved ones were filled with gladness and rejoicing when they reached the grave? If they have been born again, I can assure you that their next second of life after life was glorious. Oh, how I was granted to see that my beloved son was indeed filled with joy. It would have been my choice to have been able to see this joy in his life on this side of his grave and to be able to share in it with him. Nonetheless, there was a different path that prevailed. However, with an awareness from the spiritual domain, I did get to share in it with him and will do so for all eternity.

Job's posture in grief and despair did not deny the right of his humanity to mourn. He lost ALL ten of his children at one time while they were having dinner together, BUT look at how he responded. ***"Then Job got up, tore his robe, shaved his head, fell to the ground and worshiped" (Job 1:20-21).*** He displayed the customary antics of grief for his culture, but then he did what may have seemed impossible. HE WORSHIPED!

The modern Church has adopted the idea that to be spiritually mature when dealing with death, we must deny normal human emotions such as grief and human suffering. Particularly with African American churches, there's been the adoption of calling funerals "Homegoing Services," "Celebration of Life," or other flowery titles to indicate that it is a time of joy and celebration rather than sadness and mourning. We have erroneously surmised that we have obtained a heightened spiritual plateau by having praise, worship, and fiery preaching during eulogies at funerals and even altar calls for salvation. After all, isn't this adhering to the exhortation in I Thessalonians 4 to not grieve as those who have no hope? But the answer is, "most certainly not!" Grieving and sadness are normal, and while there is certainly joy and celebration at the loved one's going to Heaven, funerals should not frown upon an individual's humanity in expressing grief.

This particular topic had come up at a grief support group that I had attended. Several of the participants had expressed their beliefs that they felt their grief process had been dealt with in suppression due to the church making them feel that as Christians, we shouldn't be sad or mourn over death. I began to think through this and my experience as a hospice nurse that allowed me to attend many funerals within different cultures. As I reflected on this, I immediately recalled the "Homegoing Service" for my former pastor and his wife that had perished together in a car accident. It was very heavy and surreal that we were staring at these double caskets and this tragedy had occurred. There was no way to hold the tears in. But I remembered the touting manner in which the preacher stood up and rebuked the congregation and family for crying, thus demanding that we celebrate and rejoice! I remember feeling a bit confused and slightly angry. I interjected this experience into the grief class and concurred that I could understand that these ladies haven't felt they had the right to grieve.

Paul does not say, "Do not grieve." Forthwith, it doesn't quantify grief but qualifies it with instructions to not grieve hopelessly like those who don't have the truth of God's word about eternal life. We have hope because if both ourselves and our loved ones have received the finished work of Christ on the cross through His life, death, and resurrection, then we will see and live with each other once again. This will occur the moment we transition from this life into the portals of Paradise for the grandest family reunion that's beyond comprehension. Or, if we are still here when Christ returns, we will meet them in the air to live in New Jerusalem on the New Earth with a New Heaven. Regardless of this hope, it doesn't remove the humanity of love and relationship that is attached to our loved ones and friends that lived this earthly life with us, and this will cause human pain and heartache.

In as much, Ecclesiastes declares that there is a time to weep and a time to laugh; a time to mourn and a time to dance. God operates in seasons and time that is void of clocks and calendars but rather occurrences in life. There's a scripture that says that weeping will endure for a night, but joy comes in the morning. The full reference of **Psalms 30:6** is about times and seasons. The weeping that comes in a season of darkness, pain, trouble, grief, representing the night, may linger for a while. We can't put a distinct timetable on the seasons, but at some point, joy will come. However, we know that the joy in the morning doesn't occur at the time the clock strikes 6 a.m. Although there have been times that I've cried myself to sleep and when I awoke the next morning, the pain seemed lighter, only to return later during the day or night. But upon that first awakening moment of the morning, it was lighter, for the season of the night was not over. ***"For His anger lasts for only a moment, His favor is for a lifetime. Weeping may stay for the night, but*** *joy comes in the morning."* The full context of the scripture that we readily quote about weeping lasting for a night is indicative of times and seasons. God's time of anger is only for a short time or season, but His favor is forever. Likewise, weeping is for a time or season, but joy will eventually return.

He accomplishes seasons with tasks and order within the confines of life's rites of passage, if you will. For example, ***"When I was a child, I spoke like a child, I thought like a child, I reasoned like a child. When I became a man, I gave up childish ways" (1 Corinthians 13:11).*** Accordingly, if we are forty years old but are still speaking and thinking in a manner as we did at ten, then we are out of time and season. Moreover, when we should be weeping and mourning but are laughing and dancing, we are out of time and season. Consequently, this can lead to very negative results in our lives. We know from a medical standpoint that suppressed or prolonged grief and other toxic emotions can lead to physical illness and disease.

Given these points, we must allow an appropriate display or season of grief when dealing with death and not believe that we are being less spiritual when we display the appropriate emotions. When Jesus was with Mary and Martha before He resurrected Lazarus from the dead, He wept as well. Many of the crowd equated Jesus' tears with how much He loved Lazarus. Yes, we may have the knowledge that someone is in a "better place," but there are a human void and heart knowledge that must heal as we learn to live without our loved one's presence. Jesus' tears were multifaceted. He also was looking intently at the human experience of death and grief. He beheld the heartache of two sisters. So, He was able to perceive the effects of loss on a family. Likewise, he felt it too. But not only was He gaining the human experience from this standpoint, He was going to experience the full magnitude of the sorrow that comes with his own impending death and dying. He had to complete the full measure of physical and spiritual death by dying, being buried, and going to Sheol for us. Jesus even displayed human concerns about suffering. After all, in His humanity, He was familiar with grief and sorrow, just as we are. *"He was a man of many sorrows and well acquainted with grief. He was despised and rejected by men, a man of sorrows, acquainted with grief"* (Isaiah 53:3).

Yet while crouched down in the Garden of Gethsemane, Jesus grappled with the weakness of His humanity for self-preservation. We idealize Jesus as a form of a Captain America/Iron Man/Hulk-like spiritual Avenger™. But we see that was not the case. Imagine His torture of crying out to His Father, "Father, is there any other way? If it is, please do it. But Father, if this is the only way; nevertheless, it is not My will, but Yours that will be done!" Let's review the exact scriptural narrative.

"Then Yeshua comes with them to a place called Gethsemane, and He tells the disciples, 'Sit here, while I go over there and pray.' And He took along Peter and Zebedee's two sons, and He began to be sorrowful and troubled. Then He tells them, 'My soul is deeply grieved, even to the point of death. Stay here and keep watch with Me.' Going a little farther, He fell face down and prayed, saying, 'My Father, if it is possible, let this cup pass from Me! Yet not as I will, but as You will.' Again for a second time He went away and prayed, saying, 'My Father, if this cannot pass away unless I drink it, let Your will be done'" (Matthew 26:36-39, 42).

The Holy Spirit revealed that this moment solidified to Christ even further why He must die on the cross and be resurrected. Christ was thinking back to Sheol, and He didn't desire for us to merely rest in peace but to have a thriving life and live abundantly with Him and the Father as it was designed to be from the beginning in Eden.

"Therefore, since the children share in flesh and blood, He Himself likewise shared the same humanity—so that through death He might break the power of the one who had the power of death (that is, the devil) and free those who by fear of death were in bondage all their lives. For surely He is not concerned about angels, but about the seed of Abraham" (Hebrews 2:14-16). Here lies the revelation of who had the power of death—the devil. Because of Christ's work on the cross, we do not have to be held captive by the fear of death any longer. Henceforth, we should be assuredly free.

All things considered, the fear of death is the most commonly shared fear regardless of culture, ethnicity, or religion. It is the root cause of most other fears. If there's a fear of snakes, it's because of the fear of getting bit and dying. If there's a fear of boats, it's because of a fear of the boat sinking and the occupants drowning. If there's a fear of heights, it's because of a fear of falling and dying. I think you get the point. Many can have such a fear, so much so that there's a diagnosis called *thanatophobia*. Thanatophobia is such an intense fear of death that it paralyzes the individual to such a degree that it affects their life. It's understandable that we may fear how we may die. After all, no one likes to entertain the thoughts of pain or suffering. I have heard many people say that they hoped to die in their sleep. Ultimately, this isn't for hope of having a great death experience. But it's the quintessential idea of sugar plum fairies dancing in our heads with thoughts of avoiding any form of suffering that will lead to our last earthly breath. However, God desires to deliver us wholly from this fear of death.

Yet because we cannot bear living life without our child, children, spouse, or parents, we fight to hold on to this earthly vessel at all costs. We may produce unnecessary suffering on our loved ones and even ourselves trying to save the human body, many times in lieu of quality of life. Many times, medical intervention will not stop death but merely prolongs the suffering of "living."

Death is the hardest and most devastating part of life, but it is not the result of a lack of faith or an unanswered prayer. The Sovereign God knows the number of all of our days. This isn't suggesting that He designed the means of death that we succumb to, but He knows what Satan will do to cause the closure of earthly life. There may not be an understanding of the "why's" to these difficult times in life, but we can understand the "how's." The "how's" of uncertainty and pain can only be found in the word of God.

"I know You can do all things, no purpose of Yours can be thwarted. You ask, 'Who is this, who darkens counsel without knowledge?' Surely I spoke without understanding, things too wonderful for me which I did not know. You said, 'Hear now, and I will speak; I will question you, and you will inform Me.' I had heard of You by the hearing of the ear; but now my eye has seen You. Therefore I despise myself, and repent on dust and ashes" (Job 42:1-6). Job was conveying that we can hear about God, and we think we trust and know Him. On the contrary, it's not until we can see Him by the Spirit that we truly know and trust Him in ALL things.

If you have accused God or perhaps have been angry with Him for a loved one's death, He understands, and He is not angry. He gave life, but He didn't take it away. We can turn those emotions towards the genuine culprit of death and thank Jesus for defeating him. If Satan's evil spirit will show up in the churches where people worship God, how much more would he attack the physical temples of God, which are our bodies? The attack of sickness, tragedy, disease, and addiction in our minds and bodies is just as much a spiritual attack as it is physical because there is an evil spirit that maligns the soul and physical health of a person. We see the results through the physical manifestations in their bodies, which could result in the cessation of physical life. This is precisely the reason that Jesus forgave sins as well when healing a person, as we see all through the Gospels.

Moreover, what Jesus did for the spirit would defeat the sting of death, hell, and the grave. **"But if Christ is in you, then even though your body is subject to death because of sin, the Spirit gives life because of righteousness. And if the Spirit of him who raised Jesus from the dead is living in you, he who raised Christ from the dead will also give life to your mortal bodies because of his Spirit who lives in you." (Romans 10-11).** Henceforth, a physical death will happen to all of us until Jesus returns. When we cease to live on earth, He will release our spirit from our body immediately into everlasting life. This is how HE conquered death. God is the greatest Conductor when we see how He orchestrated the plan for mankind to regain life forever.

Do we really comprehend the full measure of Christ's defeat over death, hell, and the grave? Job shouted these words through a time of great accusation from those around him: **"Yet I know that my Redeemer lives, and in the end, He will stand on earth. Even after my skin has been destroyed, yet in my flesh I will see God; I myself will see Him with my own eyes, I and not a stranger. My heart grows weak within me" (Job 19:25-27).** What an utterance to proclaim in the midst of it all!

Chapter 8

There's a Time for Everything Under the Sun

"Since the day of my birth, my death began its walk. It is walking toward me, without hurrying." ~ Jean Cocteau

The Ecclesiastical narrative expressed that there is a time for everything under the sun.: ***"There's a time to be born and a time to die" (Ecclesiastes 3:2).*** Whether someone is a few hours old or 100 when they pass from this life, it's never going to be the right time or enough time in our hearts and minds. Death ends the body but not the relationship, and the greater the love, the greater the pain of grief. We cannot understand why each individual has a measure of days assigned to them. But what I do know is that Satan watches for open doors in our lives that could contribute to what we determine as premature death or "dying before their time." We say this with the intent that everyone should have a long life of 70 years old or greater, but when they don't, we reckon within ourselves that they died "prematurely."

Ecclesiastes 9:12 gives us a sobering alert of just how fragile and unpredictable life is: ***"People most definitely don't really know when their time will come. Like fish tragically caught in a net or like birds trapped in a snare, so are human beings caught in a time of tragedy that suddenly falls to them."*** We have the old clichés about living life every day like it's our last. This should not be a mere expression, but rather it should be life's reality. Let's take a deeper look into the two times that are set for us: birth and death. Neither discriminates based upon any human status of race, religion, age, socio-economic status, sex, follower of Christ, or a non-follower of Christ. Life and death; one cannot happen without the other before Jesus comes.

The poetic narrative we find in **Psalms 139:13-16** paints a portrait of our spiritual existence before our earthly beginning, and the number of our days was known before we were ever born. *"For You have created my conscience. You knit me together in my mother's womb. I praise You, for I am awesomely, wonderfully made! Wonderful are Your works—and my soul knows that very well. My frame was not hidden from You when I was made in the secret place, when I was woven together in the depths of the earth. Your eyes saw me when I was unformed, and in Your book were written the days that were formed—when not one of them had come to be."* What beautiful balladry from the heart of God to His poetic prophet.

We each have an individual book of our lives with our individual stories. God is never afraid of what we may view as mistakes in the plot of life. For *"He has made everything beautiful in its time"* (***Ecclesiastes 3:11***). He even bottles each and every last tear and records them in His book. *"You keep track of all my sorrows. You have collected all my tears in your bottle. You have recorded each one in your book" (Psalm 56:8).* He leaves nothing to waste. He uses it all. He knows the end from the beginning and the beginning from the end of our lives. God was conveying that those things that are not good, like death, have been redesigned to work together for us by producing the restoration of eternal life that will cause us to never die again or, better yet, never experience the pain of our loved ones dying again. Allow me to explain.

If we have already passed into our eternal life when our loved ones pass away from earth, there won't be the pain and heartache that we once experienced before while living on earth, but there will be the joy of a lifelong family reunion. Conveying that Jesus worked death for our good is NOT conferring that death itself is good because it's an enemy, according to the Bible. Also, just because we love God and are called according to His purpose doesn't mean that we will not undergo a physical death or lose loved ones to physical death. There are many great ministers, evangelists, prophets, teachers, and pastors who have died tragically, unexpectedly, and even suffered through prolonged terminal illnesses. Our humanity wants to believe that Christians are fully exempt from days of trouble, trials, and suffering, and if "we are great" in the Kingdom of God in man's eyes, then surely no harm can come to us. This is such a false narrative contrived in our minds, intending to cause confusion and ill feelings towards God.

But naturally speaking, there is good that can be brought out of pain, tragedy, and yes, even death. How many books, foundations, movements, or businesses have occurred as a result of someone's legacy after they have passed on? These things may have never occurred had it not been for the pain of a loved one's death that pushed out the beauty from the black mountain-high pile of ashes.

Joseph understood what it was like to trust in what the enemy meant for bad and God used to bring some good for His purpose. *"But Joseph said to them, 'Don't be afraid. For am I in the place of God? Yes, you yourselves planned evil against me. God planned it for good, in order to bring about what it is this day—to preserve the lives of many people'" (Genesis 50:19-20). In* addition, **Romans 8:28** exhorts us further: *"Now we know that* *all things work together for good for those who love God, who are called according to His purpose."* ALL things means *ALL*, so that includes death. We interpret this scripture inwardly as this: *"We know that all things are good, for those who love God,"* but we know logically that this is not true. All things are NOT good for us who love God, nor are ALL things good. It may appear that these different versions are all implying the same thing, but they are not.

For example, although I have always had a burning passion to become an author, I find it highly unlikely that I would have ever written about death. As a matter of fact, I didn't even want to think about death, let alone write about it. But as a result of my son's death and the associated supernatural encounters, this book was produced. Undoubtedly, my son's death was not good for me. Yet through it, something good was extracted from the tragedy.

Now a time to die, as mentioned in Ecclesiastes, is more arduous to direct our attention to. A time to die does not convey that God created or caused the circumstances that will end an earthly life. Yet in His Sovereignty, He knows when and how it will occur. We wrestle with the "what if's" that could have saved or changed the outcome of the timing or circumstances of a death, especially an unexpected death. The "what if's" will never be resolved because, my friends, it was never in our hands to control in the first place. Most certainly, we can pray and hope for someone to have a long and healthy life, but someone's life could be 100 hours or 100 years, and we are mere men and women who do not possess the power to judge or understand the purpose of either course of longevity. Ultimately, when dealing with the timing of death, it is like trying to put a fully formed butterfly back into its cocoon. We will never be able to make the timing fit into any scenario that will be determined as a good time or right time to die.

At this writing, one of the most popular contemporary Christians songs right now is entitled *Why God* by Austin French. It asks God those hard questions that many people think or have had at one time or another; However, I want to focus on the encouragement of having an honest conversation with God relative to grief or pain from loss. We may not understand the timing or perhaps the circumstances of death for a loved and may want to ask, "Why God?" But know that God's hand did not bring about what we deem as evil or bad and He did not take, slay, or kill our loved ones. What we MUST understand is that He loves us through it all, and we need Him more than ever during these difficult moments. He never wanted man to experience this fallen state of sin, which produced death. He is not afraid of our questions or dismissive of our attempts to make sense of life, death, and everything in-between. He is not afraid of our "whys." Google the lyrics to the song "Why God" by Austin French and allow those lyrics to saturate your soul. Within the next chapter lies the evidence of what sin has cost our lives in terms of life spans.

If we truly believe the Ecclesiastical narrative of seasons and time, inspired by God and written by the wisest man in the world, King Solomon, then beyond our understanding, there's truly a time to die for all of us. But I must clarify that knowing there's a season and time under heaven for everything, even death, doesn't mean that we don't pray for someone's healing or safety. Abort the seductive words and influence of the enemy to twist these words to cause the false conclusion of "Well, what's the point of praying then? "If it's their time to go, it's their time to go." Honestly, in my vulnerability of pain, Satan attempted to cause me to buy into this seductive lie. But the exaltation in **Luke 18:1** was anchored in my spirit that ***"men ought to always pray."*** We still must exercise our faith in God and His Word, but we need to know that there are going to be times that even though we do pray for someone, there still may be an outcome that we did not hope or believe for.

"I've learned over the years to appreciate God's timing, and you can't rush things; it's gonna happen exactly when it's supposed to." Sevyn Streeter.

Nothing happens until it's time. Yes, this sounds very cliché, but it is true. Recall the narrative of Abraham and Sarah when the angel of the Lord said, **"And he said, I will certainly return to thee at [this] time of the year, and behold, Sarah thy wife shall have a son" Genesis 18:10 (Darby).** We can look at **Galatians 4:4-5 (ESV)** and see that even the first coming of Christ was set at an appointed time: **"But when the fullness of time had come, God sent forth his Son, born of woman, born under the law, to redeem those who were under the law, so that we might receive adoption as sons."**

Timing for us is most palpable when it fosters births or deaths. There have been times when I have questioned God as to why someone had a child or children in unfavorable conditions or bad circumstances. But the Holy Spirit has taught me that each human life is born with a purpose despite the human conditions they are born into. He is the giver of life, and the precept to be fruitful and multiply did not come with man's accessories of thought as to what's good or bad timing or circumstances to bring a life into this world. A stern caution to man's labels of "bastard," "out of wedlock," "mistake," or "a product of sin," labels we have contrived to define a child or children who were not born in a traditional sense of social acceptance. GOD IS THE GIVER OF LIFE, PERIOD! Who are we to discount a life that contains God's breath? Nonetheless, we downtrod the child's identity based on the circumstances of their conception. We smirk and whisper as a young teenage girl walks by six-months pregnant. But allow me to throw a nugget out there.

Mary, the chosen earthen vessel to carry the Son of God, was a teenage mother. Not only that, but her pregnancy circumstances also had the makings for a great reality TV show. Nonetheless, we hold this teenage mother in high regard, to the point that an enormous religious group recites prayers to her. Yet, we degrade any other teenage mother. God designed everything about Jesus' birth to be lowly in nature to begin His human experience. He had an engaged, teenage mother. He was born in the lowest part of a house where the animals were kept. The circumstances of Jesus' conception and birth were inopportune moments based on our ideas during that ancient time and most certainly ours today.

Conversely, God's design was symbolic of Jesus' being present for us in our lowest times. His teenage mother represents all teenage or unwed mothers who have been given a life to carry but are frightened and scared. Being born in a separate room in the home where the animals were kept and laid in a manger represents the poor, broken, needy, and rejected. The drama of a mother who was carrying a child that was not her spouse's represents the embarrassing situations that men so easily judge and ridicule us for, further imploding the guilt and shame we may bear.

In conclusion, in our subjective logic, there were numerous reasons for His birth to have been thwarted to a more perfect situation such as a mature mother around 30, happily married to avoid the possibility of a scandal in attempting to explain the unexplainable conception. There was nothing easy or "perfect" in the Word being made flesh, but just as His birth and life was divine timing, so is EVERY life created by God.

"The days that were formed, when not one of them had come

to be." This is one of the hidden mysteries of our existence. During the first year of grappling with the Holy Spirit surrounding my son's death, I engaged with Him to unpack some questions, not so much about his actual death but more so about understanding death as a whole. He gave me this rather profound analogy that captured the revelation of this scripture, which I have read countless times but didn't quite grasp the full revelation that it entails. Jesus taught in parables and analogies to help us understand matters related to His Kingdom. Thus, the Holy Spirit frequently functions similarly to help us understand difficult things.

The Holy Spirit spoke these words to me about my son's life and death, and I will never forget them: *"Just as there was a date stamped on his birth certificate with his date of birth; likewise, there was an invisible stamp with his date of death known by Me, for I know all things."* Psalms 139 began to resonate like a resounding melodic symphony that orchestrated me directly into an "ah-ha" moment. "So, let me get this straight," I said to the Lord. *"The number of our days was known by You before the very moment of conception ever existed, and You know exactly how many days we all have, right?"*

"Right," He said.

"So then, why didn't You just tell me when my son was going to die?"

But in the blink of an eye, I took a deep breath and exhaled slowly as the answer immediately flooded in from the Spirit to my soul. I perceived a sense from the Holy Spirit as if I could personify Him stepping back to look at me with His hand gently clasped over His chin and posturing to give an assuring nod of protection and safety as I was about to forge head-on into my mere humanity. Sitting there like putty in His hands, I recoiled as I nodded in agreement that as his mother, I would have never been able to handle the foreknowledge of the date that my son would die. As I was thinking this through, I realized that before he was born, I never knew what the exact date of his birth would be, either. So, God was right; these dates are known only to Him. This was not to imply that there was any doubt in what He said, but only that my intellect was now able to connect to His words.

As I continued my dialogue with the Lord, I was pulled in closer to His breast to rest my head on His heart, and there I gained intrinsic credence that the Father God felt my intense pain. In as much, my pain was His pain. He loved me, and this part of life that we must suffer through was never His desire. In addition, by the Spirit of God, I began to see through His eyes, His pain as a Father who had to bear watching His first creation and then all men having to die, which caused the ultimate casualty of watching His own Son die. I just sat there in wonderment. I had never been able to perceive the heart of the Father's pain of knowing that His Son would have to take on human flesh and die for all of His children, and for their first time, He would bear the pain of separation from His Son. The indelible understanding of God as a parent was completely new territory for me, and it's very difficult to fully articulate.

Ultimately, I began to recall how God did almost everything to let me know through supernatural means, just shy of the Holy Spirit telling me directly, that my son's journey had come to an end. My son's life insurance policy expired when he was 26; henceforth, 30 days later, he expired. To credit my disdain for the instructions that kept upsetting me, I completely disobeyed the Holy Spirit that kept speaking and pushing me to obtain another life insurance policy on him. Yet, my psyche couldn't bring to the forefront of my consciousness what the Spirit was trying to prepare me for.

Consequently, I had to bury him a month later without any life insurance. I knew the voice that was speaking to me, yet like any good Christian who is told something that is too burdensome or we don't like, I began to rebuke the devil and dismiss it out of my fear.

Nonetheless, I was given a complete concourse of events that led me on a spiritual journey up until the very last 24 hours before my son's young life transitioned. As I humbly sat in awe with thoughts and memories of these events, I could only weep, but not from the pain of losing my son, but rather from a heart of adoration and thanksgiving as I reflected on the gift that was given to me by a God who truly hides me under the shadow of His wings. I didn't get to just see what happens when we die, but I got to see what happened when my very own son died!

The spiritual experiences surrounding my son's death pressed heavily on my heart like a vice gripping my chest. The resplendent visions and experiences that I had is the fruit that has produced the words for **Life, Death, and Everything In-Between**. Over the past three years, there has been a quest to examine the exceptional moments that are rehearsed in my soul like an old tape recorder being pressed to rewind over and over again. With each succession of replay, God revealed an increased depth of understanding and revelation to my questions, like following the yellow brick road in the Land of Oz. Continuing on, let's put on our ruby red pumps (or boots, if you are a man) and keep walking.

But before we follow the golden road into the wonderful land of Paradise, there needs to be an inordinate insight into two critical divine chronicles of biblical proportions:

1. Examining the afterlife before Jesus was crucified, died, and rose again.

2. Exploring the changes to the afterlife now that He has been crucified, died, and risen again.

There is an exceptional variance between the former and the latter that many may not have the spiritual understanding of, or perhaps, we may take for granted the Heaven and eternal life that we know of today. I wasn't sure exactly the purpose of the Lord leading me down this particular path on this aspect about eternal life until approximately three days ago. Then it jumped out at me while listening to a broadcast on Christian radio of a Seventh Day Adventist minister talking about the afterlife. As if someone was scraping their fingernails against a chalkboard, I heard erroneous and rather arrogant teaching on the subject. God's word has to be taken as one full story. The Old and New Testament was not two divisions or two different books but one continuous historical narrative, from the beginning to the end.

Chapter 9

If You Eat of the Tree, You Shall Truly Die

"The fall of man did not introduce evil; it placed us on the wrong side of it, under its rule, needing rescue." ~ N.D. Wilson

It's very compelling to realize that the first recorded physical death on this earth involved parents losing a child. Speaking from experience, it is a most heart-wrenching event that can produce a devastating liability for the rest of your life. Adam and Eve were experiencing how their actions now produced the manifestation of death on the earth. Unfortunately, the first family represented many aspects of life in a fallen, sinful world. The contention of sibling rivalry resulted in the unthinkable. Adam and Eve experienced death through Cain slaying Abel, and now the concept of death became a forced reality. Cain's sin of murder was the outward result of the inward consequences of his parent's sin and spiritual rebellion. Therefore, sin and death spread to all of us. *"So then, just as sin came into the world through one man and death through sin, in the same way death spread to all men because all sinned." (Romans 5:12).*

Man acquired a bill that we couldn't pay, and the wages of sin is death. But the Father and Son had a plan that would redeem man and regain eternal life. **Romans 6:23: *"For sin's payment is death, but God's gracious gift is eternal life in Messiah Yeshua*** *our Lord."* The ravages of death belong to Satan. God could not undo the physical consequences of sin and death on the human body. Our body is a complex shell with five senses and multiple organs that are constrained to this earth. It's our earth suite to house the real man, which is our spirit and soul. It's just like a jacket or overcoat. But once this body is damaged from old age, sickness, disease, or tragedy, we take it off, just like removing an overcoat when you come in from the cold. We exchange this fleshly body for our spiritual body, and we transition to live on for all eternity. Let's examine I Corinthians 15:39-50, which explores the difference between a human body and spiritual body. *"All flesh is not the same flesh, but there is one flesh of humans, another flesh of animals, another of birds, and another of fish. There are also heavenly bodies and earthly bodies, but the glory of the heavenly is one thing while the earthly is another. There is one glory of the sun, another glory of the moon, and another glory of the stars; for one star differs from another star in glory.*

So also is the resurrection of the dead:
Sown in corruption, raised in incorruption!
Sown in dishonor, raised in glory!
Sown in weakness, raised in power!
Sown a natural body, raised a spiritual body!

If there is a natural body, there is also a spiritual body. So also it is written, 'The first man, Adam, became a living soul.' The last Adam became a life-giving spirit. However, the spiritual is not first, but the natural; then the spiritual. The first man is of the earth, made of dust; the second man is from heaven.

Like the one made of dust,
  so also are those made of dust;
and like the heavenly,

so also are those who are heavenly.

And just as we have borne the image of the one made from dust, so also shall we bear[c] the image of the One from heaven.

Now I say this, brothers and sisters, that flesh and blood cannot inherit the kingdom of God, and what decays cannot inherit what does not decay."

Let's explore man's consequences of receiving death for their sin. God told man that he would surely die, but Satan convinced Adam and Eve that this was not entirely true. God drove them from the Garden of Eden not for just the sin, but so they wouldn't reach out their hands to eat from the Tree of Life and live forever in their sinful state apart from right standing with Him. *"Then Adonai Elohim said, "Behold, the man has become like one of Us, knowing good and evil. So now, in case he stretches out his hand and takes also from the Tree of Life and eats and lives forever, Adonai Elohim sent him away from the Garden of Eden, to work the ground from which he had been taken" (Genesis 3:22-23).*

Man's lifespan was substantially reduced from Adam to Noah and from Noah after the great flood. In 2016, the World Health Organization stated that the average lifespan of man was 72 years old; King David prophesied in **Psalm 90:10,** *"The span of our years is seventy—or with strength, eighty—yet at best they are trouble and sorrow. For they are soon gone, and we fly away."* Ironically, King David only lived to be 70 years old. Life expectancy has gone from almost a thousand years to an average of 70-80 years. When God said that the day that man would eat of the fruit from the Tree of Knowledge of Good and Evil, he would surely die, it was a firm irrevocable death sentence. From the moment their eyes were opened, they immediately died spiritually, and they began to die physically. Here is a synopsis of man's life span starting with the first man Adam.

Adam died at 930 years old. Methuselah died the same year the great flood came and is the oldest man that ever lived at the age of 969 years old. After the flood, Peleg is the first recorded death at age 239 years old. Noah died approximately ten years later at age 950 years old; his son Shem died at 602 years old and Ham 536 years old. I think it's interesting that Noah's two sons, who were living before the flood, had many more years than Peleg, yet considerably less than Adam, Noah, or Methuselah. Those born after the flood, such as Abraham, who died at the age of 175, and Isaac, who died at the age of 180 years old, had their life spans significantly reduced. As more sin abounded, so did sickness, disease, and death. But where sin abounds, God's grace indeed bounds more. **Romans 5:20-21: "But law came in, in order that the offence might abound; but where sin abounded grace has overabounded, in order that, even as sin has reigned in [the power of] death, so also grace might reign through righteousness to eternal life through Jesus Christ our Lord" (Darby).**

I pulled back the curtain and looked at what we call death from a different vantage point. To accomplish this, I reviewed the definition of death from a good ol' dictionary, and there were two different ones that really stood out to me.

First, death is defined as *"loss of life"* and second, it is defined as *"the permanent ending of vital processes in a cell or tissue."* I've come to learn through that vision of my son's transition, there is a death of vital processes in the body from cell and tissue demise, thus major organs. When these organs cease to function, then we have physical death of the body ONLY. But there is no loss of life. Therefore, if there is no loss of life, then there is no real such thing as death, is there? This is not a riddle or puzzle to solve. So, if you are confused, hang in there with me!

I previously mentioned that death was a spiritual experience because death is a state of transition from body to spirit. Transition is defined as *the process or a period of changing from one state or condition to another.* Life can be described as a simile of butterflies. We are like caterpillars existing on earth. Life is like a cocoon that changes us and molds us for our final state. Death is like the shedding of a cocoon. The full transition is like a beautiful butterfly that flies away in its full form and glory of what it was always meant to be.

We move from our natural earth realm back to the spirit realm from where our being started. If God knew us before we were in our mother's womb as He stated to Jeremiah, then where did He know us from? He knew us from within Himself, and He pulled us out and brought us forth to uniquely craft every one of us before nesting us in our mother's womb. ***"Before I formed you in the womb, I knew you, and before you were born, I set you apart" (Jeremiah 1:5).***

"Thus says God the Lord, Who created the heavens and stretched them out, Who spread forth the earth and that which comes from it, Who gives breath to the people on it, And spirit to those who walk on it" Isaiah 42:5 (NKJV).

When He blew His Spirit or breath in the nostrils of Adam, Adam became a living being. ***"Then Adonai Elohim formed the man out of the dust from the ground and He breathed into his nostrils a breath of life—so the man became a living being" (Genesis 2:7).***

God's Spirit is void of the boundaries of time and space. He is Alpha and Omega. Thus, that same single breath that was blown into Adam is a continuum of every physical being made in the image of God. ***"In His hand is the life of every living thing and the breath of all mankind" Job 12:10 (ESV).*** Breath is singular and not plural. One breath, which is His breath, that He blew one time into man, is in all of mankind. We have light on the earth because when He said, "Let there be light," that spoken command is still being echoed in the universe without beginning or ending to the point the universe is expanding to make room for that continued spoken word. Hallelujah! The body's original composition is from the dust and returns to dust because it's only a temporary state of existence. We are a spirit being that is borrowing an earth suit, called a body, in order to exist in this physical domain. But our breath or spirit is forever and returns back to the same Spirit Who gave it. ***Ecclesiastes 12:7 (ESV): "And the dust returns to the earth as it was, and the spirit returns to God who gave it."***

Our minds cannot envision what the process of death could possibly entail. In other words, the inconceivable feeling of the separation of the living spirit and soul from the body. Are we scared? Do we try to clinch every muscle and breath in an attempt to keep the soul and spirit buckled into the physical body? Does it hurt to separate from the only existence that we've ever known? Unfortunately, we cannot understand these physical aspects of death until, well, we die. But now, we at least have the experiences of those who have had an actual physical experience of death and can describe the instantaneous moment of being stripped from the body and into the real form of our spirit bodies.

Interestingly enough, there's a common experience with NDEs that reported no pain when their spirit left the body, regardless of what trauma or event that may have caused their death. In fact, they reported being in a lot of pain, and then, suddenly, all of the pain was gone, and they never felt so good. At that moment, most didn't realize that they had physically died. But when their spirit returned back into the broken and damaged physical body, it was immediate pain from the physical senses this body contains.

Paul's proclamations about death are quite mystifying to our logical views about how we are taught to think about death. In as much as we read scriptures such as:

"We are confident, I say, and prefer rather to be absent from the body and at home with the Lord" (2 Corinthians 5:8).

"For to me, to live is Messiah and to die is gain" (Philippians 1:21).

"I am torn between the two—having a desire to leave and be with Messiah, which is far better; yet for your sake, to remain in the body is more necessary" (Philippians 1:23-24).

WHAT! How could this be, Paul? You would prefer to die so you could live? I thought living was living, and to die was, well, not living. So what message was Paul trying to leave for us? What mindset must we shift into to gain a true understanding of life, death, and everything in-between?

"Every man must do two things alone; he must do his own believing and his own dying"– Martin Luther.

"A good name is better than precious ointment, and the day of death than the day of birth" Ecclesiastes 7:1 (ESV).

Hmm, this truly takes the Spirit of God to grasp that our day of death is better than our birth. ***Ecclesiastes 4:2*** considers the dead and confers that the dead are better off than the living: ***"So I considered the dead, who are already dead more fortunate than the living, who are still alive."*** For in death, they are free of the trouble and trials from the oppression of living. Yet, we are oppressed and depressed because we are living on without them.

But if we changed our vantage point, we could say, "Wow! They will never have to know the pain of losing someone ever again!" That's a sensational reason that can stand alone as to why the day of our death is better than our birth. Consequently, after the great loss from my son's death, I read ***Psalms 116:15: "Precious in the sight of the LORD is the death of His Saints"!***

To my grieving heart, which was crushed in spirit, soul, and body, this was too shattering to fathom that this could even be in the Bible (my initial grief-stricken reaction). It practically felt unkind to the human flesh that was writhing in pain from the piercing blow of my child's passing. I had an immense sentiment that death bore no resemblance to anything precious. Be that as it may, I found the courage to examine this scripture and inquired of the Holy Spirit to reveal the meaning of these words because it was majorly unsettling to me.

The Revealer unfolded that this was too high and lofty of a mindset for mankind to comprehend. Yet, while we are in pain from the void of our loved ones not being with us, the Father sees it as precious because they have come back home to Him; He knew us from the very beginning before we were in our mother's womb (Jeremiah 1:4-5). He explained that the scripture says that it was precious in **HIS SIGHT**, not man's. His ways are not our ways, and His thoughts are not our thoughts. ***"For as the heavens are higher than the earth, so are My ways higher than your ways and My thoughts than your thoughts" (Isaiah 55:9).*** The Holy Spirit gave me the full understanding of what He was conveying by these words, and it healed me completely. I never blamed God, nor was I ever angry with God about my son's sudden death at barely 27 years old. However, when I read that his death was PRECIOUS, I became disgruntled with God over it. Recall that when I started studying about life and death that I was a student. But now I have become a teacher. Just like Jesus started as a young child as a student in the synagogue, but when He comes back to the synagogue again, He returns as a teacher. I boldly make this claim because it has been moments such as this that the Holy Spirit so gently and patiently taught me. Allow me to teach you the lesson of Psalm 116:5.

Our limited human rationale comprehends and hears the scripture in this manner: **"Good in the sight of the Lord is the death of His saints."** Here lies the issue. *Precious.* Does NOT mean *good!* God would completely contradict Himself in Ezekiel 33:11 if He were saying "good." **"Say to them: 'As I live'—it is a declaration of Adonai— 'I have no pleasure in the death of the wicked, but that the wicked turn from his way and live. Return, return from your evil ways. Why will you die, O house of Israel?'"** Understandably, He still applies this to all of mankind, both Jew and Gentile.

Precious is defined as *"an object, substance, or resource of great value; not to be wasted or treated carelessly."* Heaven needs nothing, just as the Garden of Eden had no need for anything. Respectfully, the only commodity that Heaven needs is His children. Jesus went and prepared a place for us.

Let's use the analogy that you prepared your home for guests by preparing the room exactly to their tastes, their favorite foods, the activities they enjoy doing, etc. Envision that you've put your whole heart into preparing your home, and you were waiting for their arrival at any moment, but then the guests decided not to come. How would that make you feel? Well, this is precisely how Jesus feels when we decide (by not accepting Him as our Savior) that we are not going to show up to the home that He prepared for us.

In the final analysis, what God was interjecting was this: "your earthly life is of great value to Me. Therefore, your earthly death will not be wasted or treated carelessly because My Son has made sure that you will have an abundant life forever, and ever now that you are finally Home in Eden. This is the summation of Psalm 116:5 that Jesus wants us to appreciate.

We see our transition as the end, the finale of life. But God sees it as the beginning of forever, the return, the perfecting of His children, no more crying, no more sickness, no more dying, truly everlasting life. If we could just renew our minds to this truth, it just may help ease some of the pain of grief. We are human, so that human soul is going to hurt. When you bury a child, it is unbearable pain. Only God sustained me. But **Romans 12:2 (NLT)** encourages us to renew our minds to what His word says. ***"Don't copy the behavior and customs of this world, but let God transform you into a new person by changing the way you think. Then you will learn to know God's will for you, which is good and pleasing and perfect."*** We cannot do this in our own strength, but it's by His power and by His strength that we can embrace this by faith, that one day we will be able to understand all things of the Spirit when we are free from the confines of humanity. With God, all things are possible.

Chapter 10

Where Do We Go from Here?

"You're trying to make sense of your world based on a very incomplete picture" ~ The Shack

The Garden of Eden was designed to be man's eternal place of fellowship and communion with The Father, Son, and Holy Spirit. As one being, all three aspects of them were present in the Garden. The Genesis biblical narrative precisely says, "Let US make man in OUR image." So, all three characteristics of God the Author, Jesus the Creator, and the Holy Spirit the Finisher spoke to Adam in the cool of the day. Another way to look at this is as follows: God thought of man; Jesus created him from the dust of the earth; the Holy Spirit finished the process by blowing a breath of life, and with all of these components, man became a living soul. How awesome is the Living I AM?

So now, sin stopped eternal life, but yet man still possessed a spirit and soul that would never die. Therefore, what happens to the spirit? As previously mentioned, there are different views and beliefs of religious denominations about the afterlife. Some believe that we are just asleep and know nothing and are literally asleep until the second coming of The Messiah. Others believe that the spirit goes to Heaven at death. The ancient religions had their own conjectures about the afterlife. Many different religions and Greek mythology have a common idea that there is some sort of afterlife for the good and the evil.

Recounting King Saul's raising the spirit of the Prophet Samuel from the dead should have been proof enough that there's no such thing as real death or total non-existence after material life is over. But what additional messages does the Bible leave us to survey the expedition of life after life? Abel's blood was spilled on the earth by his brother Cain out of jealousy of Abel's offering being received by God and Cain's being rejected. But not only was this the first death on the earth, but it was also the first edict from God which gave us a hint that there was some extent of living even though Abel's body was demised. Nonetheless, what's the mystery to be disseminated here? ***Genesis 4:8-10*** directs us to the chronicle as follows:

"Cain spoke to Abel, his brother. While they were in the field, Cain rose up against Abel, his brother, and killed him. Then Adonai said to Cain, "Where is Abel, your brother?" "I don't know," he said. "Am I my brother's keeper?" Then He said, "What have you done? The voice of your brother's blood is crying out to Me from the ground."

We are charting deep waters that require the Holy Spirit to be your lifejacket of understanding. Let's move on to dissecting the recollection of Cain and Abel.

Now, He didn't say that his blood was "like" or "seems like" it was crying out to Him. He said that "it is." This is fully stated in the present tense as a literal occurrence of action and presence that was acknowledged by the Lord. But here is the revelation. What is considered the life of our flesh? Yes, you got it, the blood! Leviticus ties in this certitude. **"For the life of the creature is in the blood, and I have given it to you on the altar to make atonement for your lives—for it is the blood that makes atonement because of the life" (Leviticus 17:11).** Therefore, the life of Abel was crying out to God. For he was abandoned to Sheol, cut off from the land of the living but yet living. God revealed the plan, but we didn't catch its gravitas. The plan was going to require a life for our lives, or to put it another way, blood for our lives was the only way to make atonement for sin. When Adam and Eve sinned, they covered themselves with fig leaves. But God took the skin of an animal, which means an animal had to die, and made coverings for their bodies. This was the very first precedent of the blood of animals being an atonement for sin. However, the blood of bulls and goats that was shed and offered up by the High Priest could no longer cleanse and satisfy the needed sacrifice for the sins of the people. ***"How much more, then, will the blood of Christ, who through the eternal Spirit offered himself unblemished to God, cleanse our consciences from acts that lead to death, so that we may serve the living God!"*** **Hebrews 9:14 (NIV).**

Furthermore, Enoch was the first person in the Old Testament who was mentioned, in any capacity of life beyond this earth, as bypassing physical death. ***Genesis 5:24 says, "And Enoch continually walked with God—then he was not there, because God took him."*** But where exactly did God take him? Both Abel and Enoch showed back up in the Faith Hall of Fame in Hebrews: God connected the dots.

Hebrews 11:4-5: "And through faith he still speaks, although he is dead. By faith Enoch was taken so as not to see death, and he was not found because God took him. For before he was taken, he was commended as pleasing to God." It was beyond miraculous all that was revealed to Enoch. We will look at his accounts about Abel and Sheol that was given to him by the archangels, Uriel and Raphael.

Chapter 11

Sheol, The First Resting Place

"But your dead will live, LORD; their bodies will rise— let those who dwell in the dust wake up and shout for joy— your dew is like the dew of the morning; the earth will give birth to her dead" (Isaiah 26:19, NIV).

Sheol was the place of departed souls before Christ's death and resurrection. It was located in the heart of the earth, and Old Testament citizens understood that both the wicked and the righteous went to this one domain of the afterlife. The accounts of Enoch and Luke mirrored each other very well, but each narrative provided different aspects of Sheol. Enoch's account actually gives four divisions of Sheol, three of them darkness and one bright. The angels that sinned with the women and bore children are bound in one division. Then there's an area for the wicked unrighteous men and the righteous. **Enoch Chapter 22 (Greek translation):** *"And thence I went to another place, and he showed me in the west [another] great and high mountain [and] of hard rock. And there were four hollow places in it, deep and very smooth: three of them were dark and one bright; and there was a fountain of water in its midst. And I said: 'How smooth are these hollow places, and deep and dark to view.' Then Raphael answered, one of the holy angels who was with me, and said unto me: 'These* *hollow places have been created for this very purpose, that the spirits of the souls of the dead should assemble therein, yea that all the souls of the children of men should assemble here. And these places have been made to receive them till the day of their judgement and till their appointed period [till the period appointed], till the great judgement (comes) upon them.'*

"I saw (the spirit of) a dead man making suit, and his voice went forth to heaven and made suit. And I asked Raphael the angel who was with me, and I said unto him: 'This spirit which maketh suit, whose is it, whose voice goeth forth and maketh suit to heaven?' And he answered me saying: 'This is the spirit which went forth from Abel, whom his brother Cain slew, and he makes his suit against him till his seed is destroyed from the face of the earth, and his seed is annihilated from amongst the seed of men."

Recall that Cain was cursed from the earth and made to be a wanderer. Cain's son was also named Enoch but was not the same Enoch as the one who was righteous and taken to Heaven without tasting physical death.

"Then I asked regarding all the hollow places: 'Why is one separated from the other?' And he answered me saying: 'These three have been made that the spirits of the dead might be separated. And this division has been made for the spirits of the righteous, in which there is the bright spring of water." In Luke 16, the rich man in torment asked Abraham if Lazarus could just dip his finger in water to cool the tip of his tongue. Now we see where the water came from, and it was not symbolic.

"And this has been made for sinners when they die and are buried in the earth and judgement has not been executed on them in their lifetime. Here their spirits shall be set apart in this great

pain, till the great day of judgement, scourgings, and torments of the accursed for ever, so that (there maybe) retribution for their spirits. There He shall bind them forever. And this division has been made for the spirits of those who make their suit, who make disclosures concerning their destruction, when they were slain in the days of the sinners. And this has been made for the spirits of men who shall not be righteous but sinners, who are godless, and of the lawless they shall be companions: but their spirits shall not be punished in the day of judgement nor shall they be raised from thence. Then I blessed the Lord of Glory and said: 'Blessed art Thou, Lord of righteousness, who rulest over the world.'"

We will see in the following paragraphs that Jesus went and preached to the souls in Sheol, and only the holy and righteous were raised during the first judgment and resurrection. Enoch 23 goes on to describe the burning part of Sheol—which is hell—where the fire never stops burning and was made for the angels who rebelled with Satan. *"From thence I went to another place to the west of the ends of the earth. And I saw a burning fire which ran without resting, and paused not from its course day or night but (ran) regularly. And I asked saying: 'What is this which rests not?' Then Raguel, one of the holy angels who was with me, answered me and said unto me: 'This course of fire which thou hast seen is the fire in the west which persecutes all the luminaries of heaven.'"*

Recall when we addressed Hell, it wasn't created for man but for Satan and his angels? To refresh our memory and connect these dots, here is **Matthew 25:41 (ESV)** again: *"Then he will say to those on his left, 'Depart from me, you cursed, into the eternal fire prepared for the devil and his angels."* Also, we have Jude as a record that correlates with Enoch. *"Though you already* *know all this, I want to remind you that the Lord at one time delivered his people out of Egypt, but later destroyed those who did not believe. And the angels who did not keep their positions of authority but abandoned their proper dwelling—these he has kept in darkness, bound with everlasting chains for judgment on the great Day. In a similar way, Sodom and Gomorrah and the surrounding towns gave themselves up to sexual immorality and perversion. They serve as an example of those who suffer the punishment of eternal fire."* **Jude 5-7 (NIV).**

It is my hope that by the end of this book, you can clench onto the understanding that the holy scriptures were meant to be one continuous story and one book. The great apocryphal books are vital to the full story, yet they were left out of the biblical canon but have been labeled as "For Profitable Reading" in the Jewish Septuagint.

The Holy Spirit inspired the Apostle Luke to write the revelation of what was in Sheol so we could see how the extraordinary work on the cross gave the ability of our departed souls to go to Heaven above, with the Lord. This is the most compelling narrative from the Lord of what eternal life consisted of before Christ. Had He not died and defeated death, this would have been our station in the everlasting afterlife. But Sheol was not good enough for Them, meaning Father, Son, Holy Spirit. Hallelujah!

Sheol was divided by two great chasms: one called Paradise, also known as the Bosom of Abraham, and the other, Hades. This is most clearly referenced in **Luke 16:19- 29 (NIV)**, the account of Lazarus and the rich man. Being a physician, Luke was very detail oriented. The Holy Spirit knew exactly which apostle to give this revelation to. This would be an exhaustive narrative revealing that after the separation from the body, the living spirit and soul lives on, thus, an undeniable afterlife. Also, this account revealed that there was a separation between the wicked and righteous as many believed. Paul asked the people in Corinth, "What fellowship does life have with darkness?" Therefore, there could have never been oneness in Sheol, as we saw in the exhaustive narrative in Enoch.

"There was a rich man who was dressed in purple and fine linen and lived in luxury every day. At his gate was laid a beggar named Lazarus, covered with sores and longing to eat what fell from the rich man's table. Even the dogs came and licked his sores. The time came when the beggar died and the angels carried him to Abraham's side. The rich man also died and was buried. In Hades, where he was in torment, he looked up and saw Abraham far away, with Lazarus by his side. So he called to him, 'Father Abraham, have pity on me and send Lazarus to dip the tip of his finger in water and cool my tongue, because I am in agony in this fire.' But Abraham replied, 'Son, remember that in your lifetime you received your good things, while Lazarus received bad things, but now he is comforted here and you are in agony. And besides all this, between us and you a great chasm has been set in place, so that those who want to go from here to you cannot, nor can anyone cross over from there to us.' He answered, 'Then I beg you, father, send Lazarus to my family, for I have five brothers. Let him warn them, so that they will not also come to this place of torment.' Abraham replied, 'They have Moses and the Prophets; let them listen to them.'"

There is nothing figurative about these tenets describing what life on the other side was like. The two domains of the afterlife were real places; however, we have something exceedingly greater now that we get to go to Heaven. Here are some notable principles from this account that we need to recognize.

Please understand that being wealthy is not bad, nor does it cause you to be a wicked person. The Bible is not expressive about this, but I understand by the Spirit that the rich man never looked at Lazarus in the eye or gave a thought or care about helping him or the poor. God always looks at the intent of our hearts. This is what Jesus was referring to when He told the rich man to sell all of his wealth and follow Him. But the rich man became very sad at these words. The point that Jesus was making was that we must be willing to let all of the temporary things of this life go, even material wealth, if necessary, in order to prepare for the greater things of our eternal life. ***"It is easier for a camel to go through the eye of a needle, than for a rich man to enter the kingdom of God" (Mark 10:25).*** Now let's press on to subjugate the narrative of Sheol.

The first principle is that we possess the full memories of our life on earth, including our families. Their consciousness is superbly intact. Second, the angels escorted Lazarus to the Bosom of Abraham, but the rich man was buried. Remember that second death that I previously spoke of? His spirit wasn't transitioning to another form of life, only eternal death. He was in torment in the fire; thus, there was no peace, serenity, rest, or calm, but only pain and suffering.

Extraordinarily, the functions that were part of our physical body, such as seeing, hearing, touching, tasting, pain, sensations, and speaking, don't stop existing in the spirit either. However, the spiritual abilities are greater than the natural body's. We know this because although there was a great separation between the two sides, the rich man and Abraham could see, hear, and talk to each other while physically far apart. Our spiritual being mirrors our earthly physical appearance, so, therefore, we recognize each other just as we do on earth. The narrative is clear, without any doubt, that the rich man recognized and knew Lazarus just as he did on earth.

The rich man had overwhelming regret for how he treated his life and others and asked Abraham to go and warn his brothers that this place was real and beg them not to come there. It is explicit that there's life after life, but it's up to us as to the nature of it. Just as Abraham told the rich man that his brothers had the Law and the Prophets, we are without excuse as well because we have the Gospel that was canonized into a book that is accessible to anyone.

Psalm prophecies that Jesus would conquer Sheol. Moreover, He would not be abandoned there, nor would His body suffer decay. ***"For You will not abandon my soul to Sheol, nor will You let Your Holy One see decay."*** **Psalm 16:10 (BSB)**. The only logical way this prophecy could be fulfilled is if Christ's body would be resurrected; otherwise, flesh decays and returns to dust; even His would have because He was flesh and bone.

Consequently, when He was beaten and died, He did so as a human being. He had real physical flesh, bones, muscles, tendons, cartilage, organs, and senses just like we have. Let's remove from our minds the false narrative that He somehow endured beatings and crucifixion without pain or real suffering because He was God in the flesh. Here is a quick overview of what was done to His flesh for you and me.

"Some began to spit on Him, to blindfold Him, and to beat Him with their fists, saying, 'Prophesy!' Also the guards slapped Him around" (Mark 14:65).

"They kept beating His head with a reed, and spitting on Him, and kneeling and bowing before Him" **Mark 15:19**.

"Then Pilate took Yeshua and had Him scourged. The

soldiers twisted together a crown of thorns and put it on His head, and dressed Him in a purple robe. They kept coming up to Him, saying, 'Hail, King of the Jews!' and slapping Him over and over" (**John 19:1-3**). He endured this as a man and was buried as one.

The fate of the millennia generations prior to Christ's death and resurrection was said to be "gathered to their people," according to Moses. According to two biblical narratives, Enoch and Elijah were the only biblical figures to not be removed from this earth through physical death but were taken directly to heaven. However, Moses has a very interesting account that we will address.

In Elijah's account, it distinctly states that he was taken up to heaven. **2 Kings 2:11:** *"Then it happened, as they continued on and talked, that suddenly a chariot of fire appeared with horses of fire, and separated the two of them; and Elijah went up by a whirlwind into heaven."* Now, we don't know why God allowed these two prophets to be taken in this manner, but biblical scholars propose that they will be the two witnesses in the Book of Revelation that will prophesy for 1260 days in sackcloth. They are eventually killed but are resurrected in three days and are taken up to Heaven in a cloud (**Revelation 11**). But if you look at *11:6 (NIV)*, the characteristics of the two witnesses' spiritual abilities clearly describe Elijah and Moses. *"They have power to shut up the heavens so that it will not rain during the time they are prophesying; and they have power to turn the waters into blood and to strike the earth with every kind of plague as often as they want."* We explicitly know that Elijah commanded the rain to stop, thus shutting up the heaven so that no rain would fall. *I Kings 17:1 (NIV)*: *"Now Elijah the Tishbite was a prophet from the settlers in Gilead. 'I serve the Lord, the God of Israel,' Elijah* said to Ahab. *'As surely as the Lord lives, no rain or dew will fall during the next few years unless I command it.'"* We also explicitly know that it was Moses who used his staff and turned the Egyptian waters into blood with a numerous amount of other plagues in the Book of **Deuteronomy 34:10-12 *"Since then, no prophet has risen in Israel like Moses, whom the Lord knew face to face, who did all those signs and wonders the Lord sent him to do in Egypt—to Pharaoh and to all his officials and to his whole land. For no one has ever shown the mighty power or performed the awesome deeds that Moses did in the sight of all Israel."***

But with Moses, what is so incredible is that God Himself buried Moses, and the Bible says that to this day, no one knows where his grave is. Not only that, Moses didn't die of old age or sickness. God just took his spirit from him at 120 years old. At this time, the average lifespan was around 600 years, so Moses was very young. **Deuteronomy 34:5-7 (NIV): *"And Moses the servant of the Lord died there in Moab, as the Lord had said. He buried him in Moab, in the valley opposite Beth Peor, but to this day no one knows where his grave is. Moses was a hundred and twenty years old when he died, yet his eyes were not weak nor his strength gone."*** It is disclosed in Jude that the Archangel Michael was fighting with the devil over Moses' body. But let's continue in this vein and allow the discernment and revelation from the Holy Spirit to continue to unfold the full picture.

Add the narrative of the Transfiguration of Jesus to the previous scriptures of the foundation of Moses and Elijah's lives and deaths. Scriptural basis is always the credibility that we align revelation with. ***"And after six days Jesus took with him Peter and James and John, and led them up a high mountain by themselves. And he was transfigured before them, and his clothes became radiant, intensely*** *white, as no one on earth could bleach them. And there appeared to them <u>Elijah with Moses, and they were talking with Jesus.</u> And Peter said to Jesus, 'Rabbi, it is good that we are here. Let us make three tents, one for you and one for Moses and one for Elijah.' For he did not know what to say, for they were terrified. And a cloud overshadowed them, and a voice came out of the cloud, 'This is my beloved Son; listen to him.' And suddenly, looking around, they no longer saw anyone with them but Jesus only. And as they were coming down the mountain, he charged them to tell no one what they had seen, until the Son of Man had risen from the dead. So they kept the matter to themselves, questioning what this rising from the dead might mean."* Definitely, Elijah went to heaven, but if the spirit is asleep, as some denominations presume to believe, then how could Moses have appeared alive with Elijah to talk to Jesus? Or if there is no afterlife, why then is the Old Testament and the lost books of the Dead Sea Scrolls like Enoch and Jasher so rich with historical portraits of life after death?

I do not like to conjecture theories without sound biblical references. But perhaps Moses didn't go to Paradise in Sheol after God buried him but was one of the few like Elijah and Enoch that was allowed to go live in heaven. I ponder this because he appeared with Elijah to converse with Jesus. The disciples recognized and understood who those two ancient prophets were completely by the Spirit of God. They didn't have Facebook, YouTube, or even photos during his time. But the point is that over 2000 years later, these common men knew exactly whom the two men were with Jesus and, yes, they were very frightened by this event.

However, before Jesus could complete and finish the work, He had to die and go to Sheol! Every sin that you could possibly think of, He bore physically, mentally, emotionally, and spiritually. For

Sheol, The First Resting Place

the first time in His temporary human existence, He experienced separation from The Father due to OUR sins. He cried out on the cross, *"Eli, Eli, lema sabachthani"?* This was Aramaic, meaning, *"Father, Father, why have You forsaken Me"?* What anguish He felt! This anguish and brokenness of spirit and soul are what Adam and Eve bore when their fellowship was cut off from the Divinity. The burden of our sins caused Him to give into death and give up His spirit. Jesus likely died of not only the physical assaults of the crucifixion but a combination of a broken heart from the separation from His Father and the effects of sin on the body. The Holy Spirit reminded me of Solomon's words in **Proverbs 18:14: "A person's spirit can sustain him when ill, but a crushed spirit — who can bear it?"**

Perhaps a crushed spirit was what caused Him to die so much faster than the other two criminals that He was crucified in the middle of. The Bible specifically demonstrates that HE gave up His life and willed His last breath. **"And Yeshua called out in a loud voice and he said, 'My Father, into your hands I lay down my spirit.' He said this and he expired."** Luke 23:46 *(ABPE)*. He was crucified like a criminal, yet He was treated differently in order that the scripture may be fulfilled. As the religious men were anxious about their high Sabbath approaching, they wanted to have the bodies removed before sunset. To speed up the death process, the Romans would break the legs of crucified victims so they couldn't lift their bodies up to breathe, which hastened their deaths. So, the soldiers began to break their legs. *But*, they came to Jesus and fulfilled **Psalms 34:21**. Let's look at the full account **"The righteous cry out and Adonai hears, and delivers them from all their troubles. Adonai is close to the brokenhearted, and saves those crushed in spirit. Many are the distresses of the righteous,** *but Adonai delivers him out of them all. He keeps all his bones—not one of them is broken."*

Indeed, Jesus was crushed in spirit, and He was perfectly righteous, so God delivered Him and didn't allow His bones to be broken, just as King David so prophetically echoed.

"So the soldiers came and broke the legs of the first and then the other who had been executed with Yeshua. Now when they came to Yeshua and saw that He was already dead, they did not break His legs. But one of the soldiers pierced His side with a spear, and immediately blood and water came out. He who has seen it has testified, and his testimony is true. He knows that he is telling the truth, so that you also may believe. These things happened so that the Scripture would be fulfilled, 'Not a bone of His shall be broken.'" (John 19:32-36).

Jesus, through His sacrifice, possessed all authority and power over Sheol and preached the gospel to those who were dead according to their flesh but who were actually alive by their spirit and souls and able to hear His teaching. Recall the account of Lazarus and the rich man as previously discussed. Scripture explains in **I Peter 3:18-19-20:** *"For Messiah once suffered for sins also—the righteous for the unrighteous—in order to bring you to God. He was put to death in the flesh, but made alive by the Ruach (Hebrew for Spirit). Through the Ruach He also went and preached to the spirits in prison. Long ago they disobeyed while God kept waiting patiently, in the days of Noah as the ark was being built. In that ark a few (that is, eight souls) were brought safely through water."*

I Peter 4:5-6: *"But they will have to give an account to the One who stands ready to judge the living and the dead. For this was the reason the Good News was proclaimed even to those now dead, so that though they are judged in the flesh before humans, they might live in the Ruach before God."*

Hallelujah! Yeshua means "is salvation." He is the Savior. He preached the Gospel to the captives in Sheol, just as He did on the earth in the land of Israel. Think about that. Don't deem this as some fictional Bible story full of symbolism and metaphors. It was a real event that was attached to the crucifixion, death, and resurrection of the Messiah! Elohim completes all things in full measure.

What jubilation this must have brought the Old Testament saints and prophets in Paradise who were foretold of this redemption plan of God that would take away the sins of the world and bring us back to right fellowship with the Father. Just envision their wide eyes stretched in astonishment as they beheld the Messiah who began to preach just as He did that day in the synagogue when He said: *"The Spirit of the Lord is on Me, because He has anointed Me to preach good news to the poor. He has sent Me to proclaim deliverance to the captives and recovery of sight to the blind, to release the oppressed to proclaim the year of the Lord's favor. Today, this scripture is fulfilled in your hearing" Luke 4:19-21 (NIV).* Conceptualize the unspeakable exhilaration as the Prophet Isaiah beheld the One whom he prophesied these words about: *"Who has believed what he has heard from us? And to whom has the arm of the Lord been revealed? For he grew up before him like a young plant, and like a root out of dry ground; he had no form or majesty that we should look at him, and no beauty that we should desire him. He was despised and rejected by men; a man of sorrows, and acquainted with grief; and as one from whom men hide their faces he was despised, and we esteemed him not. Surely he has borne our griefs and carried our sorrows;*

yet we esteemed him stricken, smitten by God, and afflicted. But he was wounded for our transgressions; he was crushed for our iniquities; upon him was the chastisement that brought us peace, and with his stripes we are healed" (Isaiah 53:1-12).

This was a prophecy about the Messiah. Now here in Sheol, face to face, "alas! He is here!" Isaiah must have thought. Furthermore, envision the reverent wonder of the Patriarchs Abraham, Isaac, and Jacob, who listened to the gospel message being preached to them in Sheol by Yeshua. Jesus was the Torah made flesh.

On the contrary, what agony must have overtaken those in Hades as they remembered how they didn't listen to Noah, Moses, and the Prophets just as the rich man had great remorse for his life on earth. There was all of mankind that died in the flood, except for Noah and his immediate family. Then those in the wilderness that rebelled against God. Likewise, the destruction of those who shut their ears and stoned the prophets and the wickedness of Sodom and Gomorrah; all now there in Sheol. Yet, Jesus preached the Good News to them still.

The Bible is more superb than any fictional mystery or science fiction novel than you could ever read and much more captivating because it is real. Now, stretch your imagination and go with me to the time of utter chaos for the Pharisees, the Sadducees, Pilate, the Roman Officers, the Disciples, all of the Marys, and every other citizen that was in an uproar about the crucified Yeshua, King of the Jews. *"And Yeshua cried out again with a loud voice and gave up His spirit. And behold, the curtain of the Temple was split in two, from top to bottom. And the earth quaked and rocks were split apart. And the tombs were opened, and many bodies of the kedoshim (Hebrew for holy ones) who were sleeping were raised to life. And coming forth out of the tombs after His resurrection, they went into the holy city and appeared to many"* (Matthew 27:50-53).

Whoa! Here was a society that was very fearful of supernatural occurrences that were largely worked by pagans rather than the Jews. There were arguments amongst the main religious Jewish groups about death and the afterlife. Now you have tombs of the dead breaking open and the dead getting up and walking around and appearing to others! It is tempting to envision the latest zombie apocalyptic sci-fi movie. But this was resurrected men and women from Sheol in glorified bodies, but yet recognizable to others. Keep in mind, this was an eye-witness account. I know by the revelation of the Spirit that the ones who actually appeared to many were not just any average people, but significant ones that would have clutched the people's attention and shook them to their core such as Abraham, Isaac, Jacob, David, Isaiah, Jeremiah, Daniel, Elisha, and Noah—all of these holy men that have been held in Sheol until the time that Yeshua would come to the earth and liberate it. Seneca Sodi's conversation with Abraham during his 40 days in Paradise references this event. Abraham confirms that he was one of the souls that was resurrected and liberated from Sheol. *"The church on earth and in heaven will soon unite in one great jubilee and celebrate the final and great victories of the cross of our Lord, at the resurrection of all the saints, from the days of Abel to the end of the age. The living saints of earth as you know will all be changed in a moment, in the twinkling of an eye, and with divine permission and arrangement, we in heaven will all go back to the cradle of our nativity and say good morning to the church on earth. Then the great resurrection shall occur. Then will follow the earth's great Sabbath. Although we have been here for long ages, yet we have looked with great interest towards this event. Tender memories cluster about the scenes of childhood and early youth, and we feel glad to know we shall soon visit the place of our early experience in the world and the scenes that witnessed our salvation from sin. And then we shall receive the fullness and completion of our salvation. The redemption of our bodies. A very few of us have already had our resurrection as you see in my own case."*

"'I have been waiting for some time to ask,' I replied, 'what made the great difference between your appearance and those other happy spirits and even my own?'

"'All the elders,' said he, 'received their resurrection at the time our Lord was raised and with Him became the first fruits of those who slept; yet we ourselves shall be freshly arrayed along with you for the marriage of the Lamb, a great event to which we all are looking.'"

Isaiah's prophecy had come to pass as written in **Isaiah 26:19**: *"But your dead will live, LORD; their bodies will rise— let those who dwell in the dust wake up and shout for joy."* Sheol has been liberated! Christ went to Sheol and took the keys of death, hell, and the grave. Although it is easy for the western mind to picture a large set of iron keys that Jesus went and grabbed out of Satan's hands, the keys represent power and authority; thus, the power to open and shut. (Strong's Lexicon Greek 2807). ***Revelation 1:18 (NIV):*** *"Jesus also took the keys of death, hell, and the grave. When I saw him, I fell at his feet as though dead. But he laid his right hand on me, saying, 'Fear not, I am the first and the last, and the living one. I died, and behold I am alive forevermore, and I have the keys of Death and Hades.'"*

Now not only do we have this astounding historical event coinciding with Jesus' resurrection, Jesus, Himself also appeared to others in addition to the disciples. *"That Christ died for our sins in accordance with the Scriptures, that he was buried, that he was raised on the third day in accordance with the Scriptures, and that he appeared to Cephas, then to the twelve. Then he appeared to more than five hundred brothers at one time, most of whom are still alive, though some have fallen asleep. Then he appeared to James, then to all the apostles"* **I Corinthians 15:3-7 (ESV).** Jesus' death was more troubling than His life. For they had killed the Son of God. *"When the centurion and those with him who were guarding Jesus saw the earthquake and all that had happened, they were terrified and said, 'Truly this was the Son of God'"* **Matthew 27:54 (BSB).** So, you see that everything that was foretold about Him, He accomplished! Praise God! *"Jesus said to them, "These are the words I spoke to you while I was still with you: Everything must be fulfilled that is written about Me in the Law of Moses, the Prophets, and the Psalms"* **Luke 24:44 (BSB).**

So, now that we see that Jesus liberated Sheol by the power of His Resurrection, what did that mean for us? What truly was meant by Him being The Resurrection and The Life? What was He making new? Yeshua is the Creator and never does the same thing twice. For example, He came through the womb of a woman, but when He comes again, He will descend from the clouds. When He came the first time, it was quietly as a baby in a manger. But when He comes the second and last time, He is coming with a loud shout as a Ruler and King.

In preparation for my next book, I have been doing extensive research on the Apocrypha, which I previously mentioned that I would be referencing from. I could have not asked for a more reassuring book than the Gospel of Nicodemus, previously called *The Acts of Pontius Pilate*. I can surely understand why many of these books were considered hidden because the information uncovers much of what the Jewish scribes would desire to remain covered. Just a brief background. This the account of Joseph of Arimathea, Nicodemus, and the high priest investigating the news that Jesus is alive and that graves have burst open and those that were dead had been seen in Jerusalem walking around. There's nothing more befitting to end this chapter with than this biblical text.

Gospel of Nicodemus, Chapter XII, verses 13-25

"Then Joseph rising up. said to Annas and Caiaphas, Ye may be justly under a great surprise, that you have been told, that Jesus is alive, and gone up to heaven. It is indeed a thing really surprising, that he should not only himself arise from the dead, but also raise others from their graves, who have been seen by many in Jerusalem. And now hear me a little: We all knew the blessed Simeon, the high-priest, who took Jesus when an infant into his arms in the temple. This same Simeon had two sons of his own, and we were all present at their death and funeral. Go therefore and see their tombs, for these are open, and they are risen: and behold, they are in the city of Arimathæa, spending their time together in offices of devotion. Some, indeed, have heard the sound of their voices in prayer, but they will not discourse with any one, but they continue as mute as dead men.

"But come, let us go to them, and behave ourselves towards them with all due respect and caution. And if we can bring them to swear, perhaps they will tell us some of the mysteries of their resurrection. When the Jews heard this, they were exceedingly rejoiced. Then Annas and Caiaphas, Nicodemus, Joseph, and Gamaliel, went to Arimathea, but did not find them in their graves; but walking about the city, they bound them on their

bended knees at their devotions: Then saluting them with all respect and deference to God, they brought them to the synagogue at Jerusalem: and having shut the gates, they took the book of the law of the Lord, And putting it in their hands, swore them by God Adonai, and the God of Israel, who spake to our fathers by the law and the prophets, saying, If ye believe him who raised you from the dead, to be Jesus, tell us what ye have seen, and how ye were raised from the dead. Charinus and Lenthius, the two sons of Simeon, trembled when they heard these things, and were disturbed, and groaned; and at the same time looking up to heaven, they made the sign of the cross with their fingers on their tongues.

"And immediately they spake, and said, Give each of us some paper, and we will write down for you all those things which we have seen. And they each sat down and wrote, saying:"

Chapter XIII. The narrative of Charinus and Lenthius commences. 3 A great light in hell. 7 Simeon arrives, and announces the coming of Christ.

"O LORD Jesus and Father, who art God, also the resurrection and life of the dead, give us leave to declare thy mysteries, which we saw after death, belonging to thy cross; for we are sworn by thy name. For thou hast forbid thy servants to declare the secret things, which were wrought by thy divine power in hell. When we were placed with our fathers in the depth of hell, in the blackness of darkness, on a sudden there appeared the colour of the sun like gold, and a substantial purple-coloured light enlightening the place.

"Presently upon this, Adam, the father of all mankind, with all the patriarchs and prophets, rejoiced and said, That light is *the author of everlasting light, who hath promised to translate us to everlasting light. Then Isaiah the prophet cried out, and said, This is the light of the Father, and the Son of God, according to my prophecy, when I was alive upon earth. The land of Zabulon, and the land of Nephthalim beyond Jordan, a people who walked in darkness, saw a great light; and to them who dwelled in the region of the shadow of death, light is arisen. And now he is come, and hath enlightened us who sat in death. And while we were all rejoicing in the light which shone upon us, our father Simeon came among us, and congratulating all the company, said, Glorify the Lord Jesus Christ the Son of God. Whom I took up in my arms when an infant in the temple, and being moved by the Holy Ghost, said to him, and acknowledged, That now mine eyes have seen thy salvation, which thou hast prepared before the face of all people, a light to enlighten the Gentiles and the glory of thy people Israel. All the saints who were in the depth of hell, hearing this, rejoiced the more. Afterwards there came forth one like a little hermit, and was asked by every one, Who art thou? To which he replied, I am the voice of one crying in the wilderness, John the Baptist, and the prophet of the Most High, who went before his coming to prepare his way, to give the knowledge of salvation to his people for the forgiveness of sins. And I John, when I saw Jesus coming to me, being moved by the Holy Ghost, I said, Behold the Lamb of God, behold him who takes away the sins of the world. And I baptized him in the river Jordan, and saw the Holy Ghost descending upon him in the form of a dove, and heard a voice from heaven, saying, This is my beloved Son, in whom I am well pleased."*

Let me pause for a moment to convey how excited I was when I read this. When I wrote earlier how Isaiah must have felt when He saw Jesus and said alas, He is here, I only saw this by the Spirit of God. I did not have the knowledge of this part of the scriptures at that time. However, it was almost exactly what I saw revealed to me by the Holy Spirit. So here now, I have the account of this discussion and activity in Sheol or hell that took place. For the sake of time, I attempted to shorten what I included, but I felt the urging of the Holy Spirit leading to present the whole account because most readers will have never heard or read this truth because it has been concealed. Trust me, it will be worth it. You will come away with a deeper and more vivid understanding of Jesus defeating death, hell, and the grave! We know that the Pharisees paid the soldiers guarding the tomb to lie and say that Jesus' disciples stole His body. So how much more would they want to keep "hidden writings" or "The Forgotten Books," another term for Apocrypha, concealed? Remember, they were the holders of our ancient scriptures. It's very difficult to not crossover into my second book. So, let's continue on with John the Baptist telling the dead that Jesus would be coming, as I try to contain my excitement!

Picking up in verse 14 of Chapter XIII:

"And now while I was going before him, I came down hither to acquaint you, that the Son of God will next visit us, and, as the day-spring from on high, will come to us, who are in darkness and the shadow of death."

Chapter XIV. Adam causes Seth to relate what he heard from Michael the archangel, when he sent him to Paradise to entreat God to anoint his head in his sickness.

"BUT when the first man our father Adam heard these things, that Jesus was baptized in Jordan, he called out to his son, Seth, and said, Declare to your sons, the patriarchs and

prophets, all those things, which thou didst hear from Michael, the archangel, when I sent thee to the gates of Paradise, to entreat God that he would anoint my head when I was sick. Then Seth, coming near to the patriarchs and prophets, said, Seth, when I was praying to God at the gates of Paradise, beheld the angel of the Lord, Michael appear unto me saying, I am sent unto thee from the Lord; I am appointed to preside over human bodies. I tell thee Seth, do not pray to God in tears, and entreat him for the oil of the tree of mercy wherewith to anoint thy father Adam for his head-ache; Because thou canst not by any means obtain it till the last day and times, namely, till five thousand and five hundred years be past."

Note: This appointed time when Messiah would come to earth states this exact number of 5500 years in the First Book of Adam and Eve and continues further in the Second Book of Adam and Eve.

"Then will Christ, the most merciful Son of God, come on earth to raise again the human body of Adam, and at the same time to raise the bodies of the dead, and when he cometh he will be baptized in Jordan: Then with the oil of his mercy he will anoint all those who believe on him; and the oil of his mercy will continue to future generations, for those who shall be born of the water and the Holy Ghost unto eternal life. And when at that time the most merciful Son of God, Christ Jesus, shall come down on earth, he will introduce our father Adam into Paradise, to the tree of mercy. When all the patriarchs and prophets heard all these things from Seth, they rejoiced more."

So here we see that Michael had told Seth the prophecy of Jesus' coming and being baptized in the Jordan. I laughed at first about the headache but then I have to understand if you have never known sickness or disease and all of a sudden you get something like a headache, I'm sure Adam felt he was dying. Physical infirmity was all new for him and he lived 930 years.

Chapter XV. Quarrel between Satan and the prince of hell concerning the expected arrival of Christ in hell.

"WHILE all the saints were rejoicing, behold Satan, the prince and captain of death, said to the prince of hell, Prepare to receive Jesus of Nazareth himself, who boasted that he was the Son of God, and yet was a man afraid of death, and said, My soul is sorrowful even to death. Besides he did many injuries to me and to many others; for those whom I made blind and lame and those also whom I tormented with several devils, he cured by his word; yea, and those whom I brought dead to thee, he by force takes away from thee. To this the prince of hell replied to Satan, Who is that so-powerful prince, and yet a man who is afraid of death? For all the potentates of the earth are subject to my power, whom thou broughtest to subjection by thy power."

We know that during Jesus' ministry, He raised the dead, healed the sick and cast out demons. Here is Satan and Beelzebub having a conversation about what Jesus did on earth and His arrival to their domain. Remember in our earlier lessons that it is Satan who kills, steals, and destroys? Well here is his written confession.

"But if he be so powerful in his human nature, I affirm to thee for truth, that he is almighty in his divine nature, and no man can resist his power. When therefore he said he was afraid of death, he designed to ensnare thee, and unhappy it will be to thee for everlasting ages. Then Satan replying, said to the prince of hell, Why didst thou express a doubt, and wast afraid to receive that Jesus of Nazareth, both thy adversary and mine?

"As for me, I tempted him and stirred up my old people the Jews with zeal and anger against him? I sharpened the spear for his suffering; I mixed the gall and vinegar, and commanded that he should drink it; I prepared the cross to crucify him, and the nails to pierce through his hands and feet; and now his death is near at hand, I will bring him hither, subject both to thee and me. Then the prince of hell answering, said, Thou saidst to me just now, that he took away the dead from me by force. They who have been kept here till they should live again upon earth, were taken away hence, not by their own power, but by prayers made to God, and their almighty God took them from me."* NOTE: This portion right here is where scholars attest that Catholics get their doctrine of praying for the dead. I will not get into this at this time in this book. But I wanted to make mention of this.

"Who then is that Jesus of Nazareth that by his word hath taken away the dead from me without prayer to God? Perhaps it is the same who took away from me Lazarus, after he had been four days dead, and did both stink and was rotten, and of whom I had possession as a dead person, yet he brought him to life again by his power. Satan answering, replied to the prince of hell, It is the very same person, Jesus of Nazareth. Which when the prince of hell heard, he said to him, I adjure thee by the powers which belong to thee and me, that thou bring him not to me. For when I heard of the power of his word, I trembled for fear, and all my impious company were at the same time disturbed;

"And we were not able to detain Lazarus, but he gave himself a shake, and with all the signs of malice, he immediately went away from us; and the very earth, in which the dead body of Lazarus was lodged, presently turned him out alive. And I know now that he is Almighty God who could perform such

things, who is mighty in his dominion, and mighty in his human nature, who is the Saviour of mankind. Bring not therefore this person hither, for he will set at liberty all those whom I hold in prison under unbelief, and bound with the fetters of their sins, and will conduct them to everlasting life."

Chapter XVI. Christ's arrival at hell-gates; the confusion thereupon. He descends into hell.

"**AND** *while Satan and the prince of hell were discoursing thus to each other, on a sudden there was a voice as of thunder and the rushing of winds, saying, Lift up your gates, O ye princes; and be ye lift up, O everlasting gates, and the King of Glory shall come in. When the prince of hell heard this, he said to Satan, Depart from me, and begone out of my habitations; if thou art a powerful warrior, fight with the King of Glory. But what hast thou to do with him? And he cast him forth from his habitations. And the prince said to his impious officers, Shut the brass gates of cruelty, and make them fast with iron bars, and fight courageously, lest we be taken captives. But when all the company of the saints heard this they spake with a loud voice of anger to the prince of hell: Open thy gates that the King of Glory may come in. And the divine prophet David, cried out saying, Did not I when on earth truly prophesy and say, O that men would praise the Lord for his goodness, and for his wonderful works to the children of men. For he hath broken the gates of brass, and cut the bars of iron in sunder. He hath taken them because of their iniquity, and because of their unrighteousness they are afflicted. After this another prophet, namely, holy Isaiah, spake in like manner to all the saints, did not I rightly prophesy to you when I was alive on earth? The dead men shall* *live, and they shall rise again who are in their graves, and they shall rejoice who are in earth; for the dew which is from the Lord shall bring deliverance to them. And I said in another place, O death, where is thy victory? O death, where is thy sting? When all the saints heard these things spoken by Isaiah, they said to the prince of hell, Open now thy gates, and take away thine iron bars; for thou wilt now be bound, and have no power. Then there was a great voice, as of the sound of thunder saying, Lift up your gates, O princes; and be ye lifted up, ye gates of hell, and the King of Glory will enter in. The prince of hell perceiving the same voice repeated, cried out as though he had been ignorant, Who is that King of Glory? David replied to the prince of hell, and said, I understand the words of that voice, because I spake them by his spirit. And now, as I have above said, I say unto thee, the Lord strong and powerful, the Lord mighty in battle: he is the King of Glory, and he is the Lord in heaven and in earth;"*

Note: Psalm 24:8 "Who is this King of glory? The Lord strong and mighty, the Lord mighty in battle"

"He hath looked down to hear the groans of the prisoners, and to set loose those that are appointed to death." NOTE: Psalm 102:19-20 "For he hath looked down from the height of his sanctuary; from heaven did the Lord behold the earth; To hear the groaning of the prisoner, to loose those that are appointed to death."

"And now, thou filthy and stinking prince of hell, open thy gates, that the King of Glory may enter in; for he is the Lord of heaven and earth. While David was saying this, the mighty Lord appeared in the form of a man, and enlightened those places which had ever before been in darkness, And broke asunder the fetters which before could not be broken; and with his invincible

power visited those who sate in the deep darkness by iniquity, and the shadow of death by sin."

Chapter XVII. Death and the devils in great horror at Christ's coming. He tramples on death, seizes the prince of hell, and takes Adam with him to heaven.

"IMPIOUS Death and her cruel officers hearing these things, were seized with fear in their several kingdoms, when they saw the clearness of the light, And Christ himself on a sudden appearing in their habitations; they cried out therefore, and said, We are bound by thee; thou seemest to intend our confusion before the Lord. Who art thou, who hast no sign of corruption, but that bright appearance which is a full proof of thy greatness, of which yet thou seemest to take no notice? Who art thou, so powerful and so weak, so great and so little, a mean and yet a soldier of the first rank, who can command in the form of a servant as a common soldier? The King of Glory, dead and alive, though once slain upon the cross? Who layest dead in the grave, and art come down alive to us, and in thy death all the creatures trembled, and all the stars were moved, and now hast thou thy liberty among the dead, and givest disturbance to our legions? Who art thou, who dost release the captives that were held in chains by original sin, and bringest them into their former liberty? Who art thou, who dost spread so glorious and divine a light over those who were made blind by the darkness of sin? In like manner all the legions of devils were seized with the like horror, and with the most submissive fear cried out, and said, Whence comes it, O thou Jesus Christ, that thou art a man so powerful and glorious in majesty, so bright as to have no spot, and so pure as to have no crime? For that lower world of earth, which

was ever till now subject to us, and from whence we received tribute, never sent us such a dead man before, never sent such presents as these to the princes of hell. Who therefore art thou, who with such courage enterest among our abodes, and art not only not afraid to threaten us with the greatest punishments, but also endeavourest to rescue all others from the chains in which we hold them? Perhaps thou art that Jesus, of whom Satan just now spoke to our prince, that by the death of the cross thou wert about to receive the power of death. Then the King of Glory trampling upon death, seized the prince of hell, deprived him of all his power, and took our earthly father Adam with him to his glory."

Chapter XVIII. Beelzebub, prince of hell, vehemently upbraids Satan for persecuting Christ and bringing him to hell. Christ gives Beelzebub dominion over Satan forever, as a recompense for taking away Adam and his sons.

"THEN the prince of hell took Satan, and with great indication said to him, O thou prince of destruction, author of Beelzebub's defeat and banishment, the scorn of God's angels and loathed by all righteous persons! What inclined thee to act thus? Thou wouldst crucify the King of Glory, and by his destruction, hast made us promises of very large advantages, but as a fool wert ignorant of what thou wast about. For behold now that Jesus of Nazareth, with the brightness of his glorious divinity, puts to flight all the horrid powers of darkness and death; He has broke down our prisons from top to bottom, dismissed all the captives, released all who were bound, and all who were wont formerly to groan under the weight of their torments have now insulted us, and we are like to be defeated by their prayers.

Our impious dominions are subdued, and no part of mankind is now left in our subjection, but on the other hand, they all boldly defy us; Though, before, the dead never durst behave themselves insolently towards us, nor, being prisoners, could ever on any occasion be merry. O Satan, thou prince of all the wicked, father of the impious and abandoned, why wouldest thou attempt this exploit, seeing our prisoners were hitherto always without the least hopes of salvation and life? But now there is not one of them does ever groan, nor is there the least appearance of a tear in any of their faces.

"O prince Satan, thou great keeper of the infernal regions, all thy advantages which thou didst acquire by the forbidden tree, and the loss of Paradise, thou hast now lost by the wood of the cross; And thy happiness all then expired, when thou didst crucify Jesus Christ the King of Glory. Thou hast acted against thine own interest and mine, as thou wilt presently perceive by those large torments and infinite punishments which thou art about to suffer. O Satan, prince of all evil, author of death, and source of all pride, thou shouldest first have inquired into the evil crimes of Jesus of Nazareth, and then thou wouldest have found that he was guilty of no fault worthy of death. Why didst thou venture, without either reason or justice, to crucify him, and hast brought down to our regions a person innocent and righteous, and thereby hast lost all the sinners, impious and unrighteous persons in the whole world? While the prince of hell was thus speaking to Satan, the King of Glory said to Beelzebub, the prince of hell, Satan, the prince shall be subject to thy dominion for ever, in the room of Adam and his righteous sons, who are mine."

Chapter XIX. Christ takes Adam by the hand, the rest of the saints join hands, and they all ascend with him to Paradise.

"THEN Jesus stretched forth his hand, and said, Come to me, all ye my saints, who were created in my image, who were condemned by the tree of forbidden fruit, and by the devil and death; Live now by the wood of my cross; the devil, the prince of this world, is overcome, and death is conquered. Then presently all the saints were joined together under the hand of the most high God; and the Lord Jesus laid hold on Adam's hand and said to him, Peace be to thee, and all thy righteous posterity, which is mine. Then Adam, casting himself at the feet of Jesus, addressed himself to him, with tears, in humble language, and a loud voice, saying, I will extol thee, O Lord, for thou hast lifted me up, and hast not made my foes to rejoice over me. O Lord my God, I cried unto thee, and thou hast healed me. O Lord thou hast brought up my soul from the grave; thou hast kept me alive, that I should not go down to the pit. Sing unto the Lord, all ye saints of his, and give thanks at the remembrance of his holiness. For his anger endureth but for a moment; in his favour is life."

Note: Psalm 30: 1-5 NIV: "I will exalt you, Lord, for you lifted me out of the depths and did not let my enemies gloat over me. Lord my God, I called to you for help, and you healed me. You, Lord, brought me up from the realm of the dead; you spared me from going down to the pit. Sing the praises of the Lord, you his faithful people; praise his holy name. For his anger lasts only a moment, but his favor lasts a lifetime." King David was more of a prophet than I ever realized.

"In like manner all the saints, prostrate at the feet of Jesus, said with one voice, Thou art come, O Redeemer of the world, and hast actually accomplished all things, which thou didst

foretell by the law and thy holy prophets. Thou hast redeemed the living by thy cross, and art come down to us, that by the death of the cross thou mightest deliver us from hell, and by thy power from death. O, Lord, as thou hast put the ensigns of thy glory in heaven, and hast set up the sign of thy redemption, even thy cross on earth! so, Lord, set the sign of the victory of thy cross in hell, that death may have dominion no longer. Then the Lord stretching forth his hand, made the sign of the cross upon Adam, and upon all his saints."

Note: Again, another doctrine that Catholics adopted of symbolizing the motions of drawing a cross on their body.

"And taking hold of Adam by his right hand, he ascended from hell, and all the saints of God followed him. Then the royal prophet David boldly cried, and said, O sing unto the Lord a new song, for he hath done marvellous things; his right hand and his holy arm have gotten him the victory. The Lord hath made known his salvation, his righteousness hath he openly shewn in the sight of the heathen. And the whole multitude of saints answered, saying, This honour have all his saints, Amen, Praise ye the Lord. Afterwards, the prophet Habakkuk cried out, and said, Thou wentest forth for the salvation of thy people, even for the salvation of thy people."

Note: Habakkuk 3:13: "Thou wentest forth for the salvation of thy people, even for salvation with thine anointed."

"And all the saints said, Blessed is he who cometh in the name of the Lord; for the Lord hath enlightened us. This is our God for ever and ever; he shall reign over us to everlasting ages, Amen. In like manner all the prophets spake the sacred things of his praise, and followed the Lord."

Chapter XX. Christ delivers Adam to Michael the archangel. They meet Enoch and Elijah in heaven, and also the blessed thief, who relates how he cares to Paradise.

"THEN the Lord holding Adam by the hand, delivered him to Michael the archangel; and he led them into Paradise, filled with mercy and glory; And two very ancient men met them, and were asked by the saints, Who are ye, who have not yet been with us in hell, and have had your bodies placed in Paradise? One of them answering, said, I am Enoch, who was translated by the word of God: and this man who is with me, is Elijah the Tishbite, who was translated in a fiery chariot. Here we have hitherto been, and have not tasted death, but are now about to return at the coming of Antichrist, being armed with divine signs and miracles, to engage with him in battle, and to be slain by him at Jerusalem, and to be taken up alive again into the clouds, after three days and a half."

It's such a pity that our modern bible doesn't have the hidden writings. There is a great debate going on about who will be the two witnesses spoken about in Revelation. Some say Moses and Elijah. Some say Enoch and Elijah because they are the two who never tasted death. The latest thing I heard was that the two witnesses represented the Christians and the Jews. However, my original belief was Moses and Elijah. But now, here it is just as plain as day without any need to try and decipher symbolism. **Revelation 11:3:** *"And I will appoint my two witnesses, and they will prophesy for 1,260 days, clothed in sackcloth."* Verses 3-12 gives the whole account that Enoch and Elijah are giving Adam and the new arrivals to Heaven.

"And while the holy Enoch and Elias were relating this, behold there came another man in a miserable figure carrying

the sign of the cross upon his shoulders. And when all the saints saw him, they said to him, Who art thou? For thy countenance is like a thief's; and why dost thou carry a cross upon thy shoulders? To which he answering, said, Ye say right, for I was a thief who committed all sorts of wickedness upon earth. And the Jews crucified me with Jesus; and I observed the surprising things which happened in the creation at the crucifixion of the Lord Jesus. And I believed him to be the Creator of all things, and the Almighty King; and I prayed to him, saying, Lord, remember me, when thou comest into thy kingdom. He presently regarded my supplication, and said to me, Verily I say unto thee, this day thou shalt be with me in Paradise. And he gave me this sign of the cross saying, Carry this, and go to Paradise; and if the angel who is the guard of Paradise will not admit thee, shew him the sign of the cross, and say unto him: Jesus Christ who is now crucified, hath sent me hither to thee. When I did this, and told the angel who is the guard of Paradise all these things, and he heard them, he presently opened the gates, introduced me, and placed me on the right-hand in Paradise, Saying, Stay here a little time, till Adam, the father of all mankind, shall enter in, with all his sons, who are the holy and righteous servants of Jesus Christ, who was crucified. When they heard all this account from the thief, all the patriarchs said with one voice, Blessed be thou, O Almighty God, the Father of everlasting goodness, and the Father of mercies, who hast shewn such favour to those who were sinners against him, and hast brought them to the mercy of Paradise, and hast placed them amidst thy large and spiritual provisions, in a spiritual and holy life. Amen."

Chapter XXI. Charinus and Lenthius being only allowed three days to remain on earth, 7 deliver in their narratives, which miraculously correspond; they vanish, 13 and Pilate records these transactions.

"THESE are the divine and sacred mysteries which we saw and heard. I, Charinus and Lenthius are not allowed to declare the other mysteries of God, as the archangel Michael ordered us, Saying, ye shall go with my brethren to Jerusalem, and shall continue in prayers, declaring and glorifying the resurrection of Jesus Christ, seeing he hath raised you from the dead at the same time with himself. And ye shall not talk with any man, but sit as dumb persons till the time come when the Lord will allow you to relate the mysteries of his divinity. The archangel Michael farther commanded us to go beyond Jordan, to an excellent and fat country, where there are many who rose from the dead along with us for the proof of the resurrection of Christ. For we have only three days allowed us from the dead, who arose to celebrate the passover of our Lord with our parents, and to bear our testimony for Christ the Lord, and we have been baptized in the holy river of Jordan. And now they are not seen by any one. This is as much as God allowed us to relate to you; give ye therefore praise and honour to him, and repent, and he will have mercy upon you. Peace be to you from the Lord God Jesus Christ, and the Saviour of us all. Amen, Amen, Amen.

"And after they had made an end of writing and had wrote in two distinct pieces of paper, Charinus gave what he wrote into the hands of Annas, and Caiaphas, and Gamaliel.

"Lenthius likewise gave what he wrote into the hands of Nicodemus and Joseph; and immediately they were changed into exceeding white forms and were seen no more. But what they had wrote was found perfectly to agree, the one not containing one letter more or less than the other. When all the assembly

of the Jews heard all these surprising relations of Charinus and Lenthius, they said to each other, Truly all these things were wrought by God, and blessed be the Lord Jesus for ever and ever, Amen. And they went about with great concern, and fear, and trembling, and smote upon their breasts and went away every one to his home. But immediately all these things which were related by the Jews in their synagogues concerning Jesus, were presently told by Joseph and Nicodemus to the governor. And Pilate wrote down all these transactions, and placed all these accounts in the public records of his hall."

Note: Pilate was Roman. As previously mentioned, the Roman Catholic Church has used this biblical text as the basis for several doctrines. In the remainder chapters, Pilate makes the High Priest show him their scroll that testifies to that which was written by Simeon's sons, such as a Messiah coming 5500 years to the earth from the fall of Adam.

I know that was a lot to digest, but I hope that it was as refreshing to you as it was for me. It connected many dots for we have such a surface level knowledge about the account of Jesus defeating death and even the grave opening up. But now, we have the deep and hidden things of God and our knowledge is increasing, just as Daniel said would happen in the end times.

Chapter 12

His Sickness Won't End in Death

"To reject this new social order was to reject Jesus, the very movement of God in flesh and blood." ~ Rob Bell

We have studied many times the account of Jesus' raising Lazarus, but has the full effect of the story been retained? It is correct that this showed the greatness of His power by raising the dead, but until we understand the background and backdrop of the account, we can't appreciate how prolific this really was. Second, when Jesus proclaimed that He was the Resurrection and the Life, how scandalous was this for the religious social order that was plotting how to stop Him? Let's travel back to Bethany and discover the answers.

Jesus beheld death from the human perspective at the time of a famous man named Lazarus' death. This was not His first acquaintance with death. His beloved earthly adoptive father, Joseph, had died at some point before Jesus was 30 years old. Lazarus was a foreshadow of His own resurrection that would pave the way to eternal life for man again. Furthermore, He was seeing the pain and grief play out in men's lives. Let's unpack the well-known biblical account in ***John 11***, with the raising of Lazarus from the dead, and review it with different-colored glasses.

First, we know that this narrative speaks of His love for Mary, Martha, and Lazarus, but more so, Mary's love for Him. This was the same Mary who will wash His feet with costly perfume and dry them with her hair shortly before His death. Second, we know that He had knowledge of Lazarus' sickness prior to his ultimate demise and remained where He was for another two days. But why was that? Surely, He loved this family, right? Perhaps when we have judged God as being late or delayed, He was only preparing an opportune time to show His glory through our situations. Martha and Mary were on the cusp of learning this lesson.

Ponder on this key reply when He was informed that Lazarus was sick. ***"When Yeshua heard this, He said, "This sickness will not end in death. It is for God's glory, so that Ben-Elohim (Son of God) may be glorified through it" (John 11:4).*** I've learned to appreciate the relatable human characteristics and often dramatic nature of the disciples. Can you imagine the looks on their faces when He decided to tarry for two more days knowing that Lazarus was sick? What mass confusion must have plagued their minds. But then things get more auspicious with the situation when He now says, "Ok boys. Let's go! Lazarus is asleep, and I'm going to go wake him up!" So, I'm sure they are scratching their heads as they thought, "Ok great, he's sleeping, so he'll be fine." They thought He was speaking of natural sleep. But He divulges that Lazarus is DEAD! For the biblical scholar who says that Jesus didn't say that, you are correct. That was the 21st-century breakdown of the following scripture to bring a modern vision of what was happening.

"After He said this, He tells them, 'Our friend Lazarus has fallen asleep, but I'm going there to wake him up.' So the disciples said to Him, 'Master, if he has fallen asleep, he will get better.' Now Yeshua had spoken about his death, but they thought He was talking about ordinary sleep. Then Yeshua told them clearly, 'Lazarus is dead! I'm glad for your sake I wasn't

there, so that you may believe. Anyway, let's go to him!' Then Thomas called the Twin, said to the other disciples, 'Let's go too, so that we may die with Him!' (John 11:11-16). Remember, in the aforementioned paragraph that I spoke of the dramatics of the disciples? Well, here is a perfect example. Now they are ready to DIE with Lazarus. Does that sound familiar to someone else they were ready to die for? But one betrays Him, and another denies Him three times.

Yet when they arrived, Lazarus had been entombed for four days. His sisters were distraught with grief. So, now we find Jesus and the disciples met by Martha, who was crushed in spirit but full of faith that Jesus had the power to do all things. *"Martha said to Yeshua, 'Master, if You had been here, my brother wouldn't have died! But I know, even now, that whatever You may ask of God, He will give You.' Yeshua said to her, 'Your brother will rise again.' Martha said to Him, 'I know, he will rise again in the resurrection on the last day.' Yeshua said to her, 'I am the resurrection and the life! Whoever believes in Me, even if he dies, shall live. And whoever lives and believes in Me shall never die. Do you believe this?' She says to Him, 'Yes, Lord, I believe that you are the Messiah, Ben-Elohim who has come into the world'* (John 11:21-28)

But what was Yeshua conveying now? Was this a well-crafted riddle: Even if we die, we live? So, therefore, if He did not die on that cross, then His profound declaration that He is the Resurrection and Life would have crumbled. Moreover, His affirmation that even when we have tasted physical death, we would still live, would have been a lie. But Glory to God! *"God is not a human who lies or a mortal who changes his mind. When he says something, he will do it; when he makes a promise, he will fulfill it"* Numbers

23:19 (CJB).

But when Martha said that she believed that Lazarus would be resurrected on the last day, this was a contentious belief during this time when there had been a long-standing belief in Sheol but no resurrection of the dead, except by witchcraft and sorcery by pagan nations.

Let's take a deep dive into understanding the mindset and culture of the two main religious groups during Jesus' time, the Pharisees and Sadducees, regarding the afterlife and resurrection. We will see just how controversial and grossly disturbing this scene of Lazarus' resurrection was for Jesus.

First, let's acknowledge that the Levitical priesthood, as outlined in the Torah or Old Testament Law, had been long forsaken due to the Jewish Diaspora or the Jews being scattered by captivity to foreign lands.

According to the Essenes, the priesthood had become a counterfeit priesthood and corrupt. The priesthood could literally be bought. Therefore, the whole temple was corrupt. The High Priest was to be from the tribe of Levi, which started with Aaron, Moses' brother, and this was to be occupied as long as the High Priest lived. Therefore, during the adulthood of Jesus, the current priesthood was not in the rightful hands of the Levites, who were to inherit this God-ordained position of the Levitical priesthood. In fact, Zacharias, the father of John the Baptist, was from the line of Levi, who was the High Priest during the birth of Jesus. Therefore, his son, John, or John the Baptizer, should have inherited the position as High Priest upon Zacharias' death. Yet we know that Caiaphas was the High Priest, who was appointed by Roman authorities and the priest who headed the trial and crucifixion of Christ. The Priest was both political and religious in their duties.

Perhaps this was the reason Jesus spoke such sharp words to the religious leaders such as found in Matthew 23:13-18:

"But woe to you, scribes and Pharisees, hypocrites! For you shut the kingdom of heaven in people's faces. For you neither enter yourselves nor allow those who would enter to go in. Woe to you, scribes and Pharisees, hypocrites! For you travel across sea and land to make a single proselyte, and when he becomes a proselyte, you make him twice as much a child of hell as yourselves.

"Woe to you, blind guides, who say, 'If anyone swears by the temple, it is nothing, but if anyone swears by the gold of the temple, he is bound by his oath.' You blind fools! For which is greater, the gold or the temple that has made the gold sacred? And you say, 'If anyone swears by the altar, it is nothing, but if anyone swears by the gift that is on the altar, he is bound by his oath.'"

The Pharisees were more liberal of their Jewish views that moved beyond the written Law of Moses. They believed not only in the immortality of the soul (the ongoing life of an individual after death) but also in the transmigration of souls. This meant that if a soul was good, it could go on and live in someone else, much like a type of reincarnation.

Now the Sadducees, on the other hand, were radically conservative in their religious views. They believed only in the written Law of Moses and rejected any later "customs" or oral traditions. So, they did not believe in any form of life after death, and there was a steady flow of contention with the Pharisees, whose progressive thinking, interpretations and additions to the law were objected to immensely.

Let's examine these narratives to create a clear picture of this division in the Temple, which is much like our modern church with the different denominations and theological disagreements. Our democracy with opposing political parties could also be compared to these two mainstream groups. I am reminded of the preacher speaking in **Ecclesiastes 1:9-10:** *"What has been is what will be, what has been done is what will be done, and there is nothing new under the sun. Is there something of which it is said, 'See, this is new'? It existed already in the ages before us."*

So, there was religious and political upheaval between the two ruling groups in the temple, and now this Holy Maverick named Yeshua, just a carpenter's son from Nazareth, has come on the scene and is vehemently opposing the status quo. Remember, **"Can anything good come from Nazareth?"** asked Nathaniel in ***John 1:46?*** Paul followed suit during the establishment of the Church as described in the following scriptural account:

"But recognizing that one group was Sadducees and the other Pharisees, Paul began crying out in the Sanhedrin, 'Brothers, I am a Pharisee, a son of Pharisees! I am on trial because of the hope of the resurrection of the dead!' When he said this, a dispute broke out between the Pharisees and Sadducees, and the assembly was divided. For the Sadducees say there is no resurrection or angel or spirit, but the Pharisees affirm them all. Then there was a great uproar" (Acts 23:6-9).

Jesus disagreed with the Sadducees because they didn't believe in the resurrection of the dead or angels or spirits. So, can you grasp how difficult it was for them to believe in Yeshua, God's Son, being made flesh? There was no understanding of spiritual things other than the Law of Moses.

***"On that day, Sadducees (who say there is no resurrection) came to Yeshua and questioned Him"* (Matthew 22:23).** Now we evidently see that there was a serious tiff between the Sadducees and Jesus about the resurrection of the dead. Be it as it may, here was Jesus not only teaching of the resurrection of the dead but stating that HE WAS the Resurrection! Moreover, He was preparing to perform a miracle that would display this very fact. So, can you presuppose the atmospheric tensions and bewilderment on that day? I can assert that it was thick with every possible human emotion known to man. So, now that we envisage the flaring nostrils on this day, allow me to return to the point when Jesus said that this sickness would not end in death.

His raising Lazarus would test and prepare the hearts of men for His own future resurrection. He foretold several times of His death, but they didn't understand. For instance, in ***John 12:24 (CJB)***, Jesus said it this way: *"Yes, indeed! I tell you that unless a grain of wheat that falls to the ground dies, it stays just a grain; but if it dies, it produces a big harvest."* However, the true revelation was that if there was physical death, life would not end from it. His death produced the big harvest of eternal life. Can you seize this enormous truth that sets us free? I appreciate the apprehension that must have just ensued, because after all, common sense tells us that if physical death occurs, then life has ended. Here lies the other side of the coin, as previously mentioned. There's a dual purpose of both the natural and the spiritual within the confines of God's workmanship. This is why He commands us to acknowledge that His will is to be done on earth as it is in Heaven. In other words, Heaven and earth should connect with one another in manifesting the plans, glory, and goodness of God! *"Remember the former things of old, For I am God, and there is no other; I am God, and there is none like Me, Declaring the end from the beginning, And from ancient times things that are not yet done, Saying,*

'My counsel shall stand, And I will do all My pleasure'" (Isaiah 46:9-10).

The Jews had never seen anyone who could heal all manners of physical and demonic infirmities, but most certainly not bringing the dead back to life.

"So Yeshua, again deeply troubled within Himself, comes to the tomb. It was a cave, and a stone was lying against it. Yeshua says, 'Roll away the stone!' Jesus was similarly given almost a play-by-play of His impending resurrection. *"They found the stone rolled away from the tomb" Luke 24:3 (NIV).* His stone was rolled away by an angel.

Martha, the dead man's sister, said to Him, 'Master, by this time he stinks! He's been dead for four days!' Yeshua says to her, 'Didn't I tell you that if you believed, you would see the glory of God?' So they rolled away the stone. Yeshua lifted up His eyes and said, 'Father, I thank you that you have heard Me. I knew that You always hear Me; but because of this crowd standing around I said it, so that they may believe that You sent Me.'" I loved the pure and honest heart that He speaks to the Father with. God wants us to come to Him in the same manner.

"And when He had said this, He cried out with a loud voice, 'Lazarus, come out!' He who had been dead came out, wrapped in burial clothes binding his hands and feet, with a cloth over his face. And Yeshua tells them, 'Cut him loose, and let him go!'"

Let's examine the revelation by substituting the word "death" in the place for Lazarus' proper name, and when we see the word "dead," we will replace it with Lazarus' name. So here is the revelatory rewrite. *"And when He had said this, He cried out with a loud voice, 'Death, come out!' He who had been Lazarus came out, wrapped in burial clothes binding death's hands and feet* *with a cloth over <u>death's</u> face. And Yeshua tells them, 'Cut <u>death</u> loose, and let <u>death</u> go!'"* The Holy Spirit just revealed to me that this was the concrete spiritual outcome of the seemingly natural occurrence of death and resurrection. God was telling us what Jesus' death and resurrection were going to do to death. When His stone was rolled away from His tomb, death was bound, and we were cut loose from its ties. To the onlookers, He was calling out a man, but to the spirit realm, He was speaking to the spirit of death. When the disciples thought that Jesus was speaking of natural sleep, Jesus was signifying that our life after death was no longer going to be just a state of rest as it was in Sheol. But it was going to be a bustle of life because HE said that He is the Resurrection and the Life. Lazarus wasn't raised to just go back and sit in the tomb and rest waiting for the Last Day. Certainly not! But yet, some religions want to teach that when we die, we are just sleeping, waiting on the Last Day because the King James version and other translations use the word "asleep" or "sleep." Yet the full context and revelation are completely misrepresented and misunderstood.

On the contrary, Lazarus was alive and living so much so that he was a local superstar and advocate of Jesus, which infuriated the religious rulers so much that they were including him in their plot to kill Jesus. They were wanting to kill the evidence of His truth, which was Lazarus. In other words, destroy the evidence of the resurrection that they didn't believe could possibly exist. *"Now a large crowd of Judeans knew He was there and came, not only for Yeshua but also to see Lazarus, whom He had raised from the dead. So the ruling kohanim (Priest) made plans to kill Lazarus also, because on account of him many of the Jewish people were going and putting their trust in Yeshua"* (John 12:9-11).

Nonetheless, I know that the disciples remembered this moment very vividly, and they passed it down through oral testimony. Case in point: Paul was not a part of the original disciples and early apostles. Conversely, he was persecuting and killing them for spreading the message of Yeshua, Son of God, and Him crucified and resurrected. However, after his Damascus Road experience and accepting the Messiah, he became one of the greatest apostles to the Church. In his letter to Thessalonica, he wrote these words: **"Now we do not want you to be uninformed, brothers and sisters, about those who are <u>asleep</u>, so that you may not grieve like the rest who have no hope." I Thessalonians 4:13 (ESV).**

The New Testament was canonized around the end of the first century AD, so Paul didn't pick up his New Testament and read John 11. Yet, here were the nuts and bolts of the same premise and vernacular of the event in John 11 spoken by Yeshua to the disciples. Do we grasp that this was radically indispensable to God for us to understand life through His Son? They not only knew of this hope, but they had also seen this hope. I am not using "seen" allegorically, metaphorically, or symbolically. But I am using "seen" to mean that they were real eyewitnesses to an event, and they were about to get two of them that dealt with death and resurrection. So, let's continue. Remember, I am taking you on a journey.

I can imagine the disciples' passion and energy from their vivid memories of that hot day in Bethany. Because when you have an undeniable encounter beyond this vortex of earthly dimension, it becomes like the old Memorex ™ cassette tape commercials. "Is it live, or is it Memorex?" Since I just truly dated myself in the mind of a clever millennial Googling all the details about this, allow me to paint a picture of one of the most famous commercials during the late 70s -90s when cassettes replaced eight-track tapes. The iconic Ella Fitzgerald would sing, and a glass would explode. The advertisement conveyed that the high quality of the cassette tape was so clear and the sound so vivid that it seemed live. The feelings, sights, sounds, words, people, colors, and emotions become a living Memorex for anyone who experienced a supernatural encounter, especially one involving Heaven or Hell.

"My friends, we want you to understand how it will be for those followers who have already died. Then you won't grieve over them and be like people who don't have any hope. We believe that Jesus died and was raised to life. We also believe that when God brings Jesus back again, he will bring with him all who had faith in Jesus before they died. Our Lord Jesus told us that when he comes, we won't go up to meet him ahead of his followers who have already died. With a loud command and with the shout of the chief angel and a blast of God's trumpet, the Lord will return from heaven. Then those who had faith in Christ before they died will be raised to life. Next, all of us who are still alive will be taken up into the clouds together with them to meet the Lord in the sky. From that time on we will all be with the Lord forever. Encourage each other with these words" (1 Thessalonians 4:13-18).

In the full account, please note that when speaking of Jesus' return, He is bringing the earthly dead with Him. *"But the men said to them, 'Why do you search for the living among the dead? He is not here, but He is risen!' (Luke 24:5-6).* Their spirits have been with Him while their bodies are decaying in the earth, returning to their original form of dust. The angels called Him the living. He paved the way for us to be living among the dead, except the biggest difference is that He took on the full resurrected body while we have to wait until He returns again to gain ours. The souls in Paradise will receive their glorified bodies in order to now live on the new earth. Those who have not had a physical death at the time of His return will be changed next and will go up to meet them in the sky with the Lord to live forever and ever. Recall Paul's words that to be absent from the body is to be present with the Lord.

Christ did a new thing for us, and He made a new heaven when He ascended back to Heaven. But we will not have the new earth until He comes back and brings the New Jerusalem down with Him, all the angels, and all the saints.

"Then I saw a new heaven and a new earth; for the first heaven and the first earth had passed away, and the sea was no more. I also saw the holy city—the New Jerusalem—coming down out of heaven from God, prepared as a bride adorned for her husband. I also heard a loud voice from the throne, saying,

'Behold, the dwelling of God is among men, and He shall tabernacle among them.

They shall be His people, and God Himself shall be among them and be their God.

He shall wipe away every tear from their eyes, and death shall be no more.

Nor shall there be mourning or crying or pain any longer, for the former things have passed away.' And the One seated upon the throne said, 'Behold, I am making all things new!' Then He said, 'Write, for these words are trustworthy and true'" (Revelation 21:1-5).

The new heaven or the new Paradise was magnificently prepared for us to live. Hallelujah! *"Do not let your heart be troubled. Trust in God; trust also in Me. In My Father's house there are many dwelling places. If it were not so, would I have told you that I am going to prepare a place for you? If I go and prepare a place for you, I will come again and take you to Myself, so that where I am you may also be. And you know the way to where I am going" (John 14:1-4).*

Everything in the Bible is significant, no matter how little or small a detail may seem. Roman crucifixion was a common practice, and often many were crucified at one time. However, God chose to allow only two other criminals to be crucified with Jesus, and this signifies evidence of the contrast between rejecting or accepting the salvation of Yeshua.

In the account when Jesus was hanging on the cross between the two thieves (who we now know their names from the Gospel of Nicodemus, Chapter 7:3, "And in like manner did they to the two thieves who were crucified with him, Dimas on his right hand and Gestas on his left"), one of them asked the Lord to remember him when He came into His Kingdom. *"Jesus replied, 'Truly I tell you, today you will be with Me in Paradise'"* (Luke 23:43, NIV). This is the word that the Lord gave me for the eulogy that I performed at my son's memorial service. I entitled it "As Long as There's Still Breath in Your Body." I will share the full details in another chapter, so remain in tune with me for a little while longer.

We clearly see that as long as there is still some breath in our body, we can call on the name of Jesus and be saved. Religion has debated and argued over "deathbed confessions" for centuries. But I implore you to recognize that one cannot be any more on their deathbed than being nailed to a Roman cross. Yet Jesus accepted the thief's, who was dying beside Him, simple request to just remember him when He comes into His Kingdom. God was allowing us to see that He looks at the condition of our inner heart more than our obvious failures. Be that as it may, the thief didn't feel he was worthy of going with Jesus to His Kingdom because of his sin. He never asked to go with Yeshua. But oh, what a Savior! That thief's belief that Jesus was who He said He was and had a Kingdom not of this earth, and this simple deathbed belief and confession got him into Paradise with The King. Hallelujah!

Religion makes things so complicated. The modern church has prepared the "Sinner's Prayer" and a systematic way that we do altar calls by having everyone bow their heads and close their eyes while the minister calls for anyone who wants to "give their hearts to Jesus or the Lord." People raise their hands as the minister loudly says, "Thank you, sir/ma'am, I see that hand." Our human nature is tempted to crack an eye open, curious who is or how many are raising their hands. Then either the minister has everyone repeat after him a prayer of salvation, or they are told to step out of their seats and come to the altar as an act of faith, showing their public confession of accepting Christ. Upon performing this traditional ritualistic plan of salvation, you are deemed to be saved.

However, this thief didn't have any such platform while dying on the cross. He only had a mustard seed of faith and a humble heart to believe in the name of the innocent Man, Yeshua, King of the Jews, hanging beside him. This is all that He requires still. He never made all of this pomp and circumstance of religion a requirement for salvation.

On the contrary, the other thief was angry, mocking, and thinking only of himself with no remorse for his actions. The repentant thief not only acknowledged his wrongdoings, he defended Jesus' against the jeering and mocking of that thief. Jesus even prayed to God and said, "Father, please forgive them for they know not what they do" (***Luke 23:39-43, NASB): "One of the criminals who were hanged there was hurling abuse at Him, saying, 'Are You not the Christ? Save Yourself and us!' But the*** *other answered, and rebuking him said, 'Do you not even fear God, since you are under the same sentence of condemnation? And we indeed are suffering justly, for we are receiving what we deserve for our deeds; but this man has done nothing wrong.' And he was saying, 'Jesus, remember me when You come in Your kingdom!' And He said to him, 'Truly I say to you, today you shall be with Me in Paradise.'"* God wanted to exemplify this stark contrast of heart.

Before the scriptures were translated, Jewish scribes didn't use punctuation but only wrote in paragraphs. Many meanings got lost in the King James translations because of our everyday use of punctuation marks. For example, look at the difference here simply based on the placement of the comma: "Jesus said, I tell you today, you will be with Me in Paradise," versus "Jesus said, I tell you, today you will be with Me in Paradise."

Thus, when Mary heard Him call her name at the empty tomb, she became overjoyed when she realized that it was her beloved Rabbi. The human emotions of seeing Him whole and healed after extensive beatings and suffering was more than she could contain. She reaches to hug Him, for I'm sure those three days and nights felt like 3,000. However, I can only imagine that He was just as eager to embrace her, but He directed her to not hang on to Him because He had not yet ascended to His Father IN HEAVEN. *"Jesus said to her, "Do not cling to me, for I have not yet ascended to the Father; but go to my brothers and say to them, 'I am ascending to my Father and your Father, to my God and your God.'" John 20:17 (ESV)*. According to the Gospel of Nicodemus, we know that the thief went to heaven ahead of Jesus and waited for Adam and the Old Testament prophets and saints to arrive in Heaven, led by Archangel Michael, not Jesus. This would correlate with His words spoken to Mary that He had not ascended to His Father yet, for we know that He was liberating Sheol from the Prince of Death.

Jesus was telling Mary that not only will He ascend to His Father, but so will all of them. Jesus was proclaiming the good news: no longer were souls abandoned to Sheol, but redemption by His resurrection has brought resurrection and eternal life for all. However, before His final and great ascension in the clouds after the great commission to the disciples was given, the discernment of scriptures guides us to another hidden gem.

During the 40 days after the Resurrection, He must have ascended to the Father at some point after His first initial encounter with Mary at the tomb. This occurred before His final ascension in the sight of the disciples. We will connect the narrative to establish this spiritual merit.

Eight days later, after He first appeared to the disciples, He allowed Thomas to *touch* Him and *feel* His wounds because Thomas was unable to accept the report from the other disciples that Yeshua was alive and had appeared to them. Mary wasn't allowed this physical contact at the time of His initial manifestation. **"Eight days later, His disciples were once again inside with the doors locked, and Thomas was with them. Jesus came and stood among them and said, 'Peace be with you.' Then Jesus said to Thomas, 'Put your finger here and look at My hands. Reach out your hand and put it into My side. Stop doubting and believe.'"** John 20:26-27 (BSB).

And also to others, He said, **"Look at my hands and my feet. It is I myself! Touch me and see; a ghost does not have flesh and bones, as you see I have." Luke 24:39 (ESV)**. What changed that now His flesh and bone could be penetrated by the human touch?

A spiritual process of ascension had transpired. So, we know that Christ ascended and descended. *"Therefore it says, 'When He went up on high, He led captive a troop of captives and gave gifts to his people.' Now what does 'He went up' mean, except that He first went down to the lower regions of the earth? The One who came down is the same One who went up far above all the heavens, in order to fill all things." (Ephesians 4:8-10).* Who was this captive troop? Allow me to provide the answer. The captive troop was the captive souls in Paradise in Sheol. Recall the graves that burst open, and the dead appeared before many? When He completed all aspects of His earthly season, He made His final ascension in the clouds to the third Heaven where the earth is its footstool. *"Knowing that the One who raised the Lord Yeshua will raise us also with Yeshua, and will bring us with you into His presence" (2 Corinthians 4:14)* The Holy Spirit desires to convey that our lives are to follow the path of Christ into the glorious realms that He began and: *"For our trouble, light and momentary, is producing for us an eternal weight of glory far beyond all comparison, as we look not at what can be seen but at what cannot be seen. For what can be seen is temporary, but what cannot be seen is eternal" (2 Corinthians 4:17-18).*

"You were buried along with Him in immersion, through which you also were raised with Him by trusting in the working of God, who raised Him from the dead. When you were dead in your sins and the uncircumcision of your flesh, God made you alive together with Him when He pardoned us all our transgressions. He wiped out the handwritten record of debts with the decrees against us, which was hostile to us. He took it away by nailing it to the cross. After disarming the principalities and powers, He made a public spectacle of them, triumphing

over them in the cross" (Colossians 2:12-15).

We are alive, although our bodies may be lying in the cold ground. I am reminded of Stephen after the crowd became enraged with his words, and he was full of the Holy Spirit, and God opened up his spiritual eyes to see into Heaven. As Stephen continued on and told them what he was seeing, they began to stone him to death, for this was complete blasphemy to the religious ears. But he asked God to receive his spirit and followed the example of Jesus by asking for forgiveness of his killers. *"The Jews and religious leaders listened to Stephen. Then they became angry and began to grind their teeth at him. He was filled with the Holy Spirit. As he looked up to heaven, he saw the shining-greatness of God and Jesus standing at the right side of God. He said, 'See! I see heaven open and the Son of Man standing at the right side of God!' While they threw stones at Stephen, he prayed, 'Lord Jesus, receive my spirit.' After that he fell on his knees and cried out with a loud voice, 'Lord, do not hold this sin against them.' When he had said this, he died." Acts 7:54-56 and 59-60 (NLT).*

God is not partial toward anyone. Just as we see with Stephen and the thief on the cross, the spirit immediately is released and transitions to be with the Lord. None of the rulers of this age understood it, *"for if they had, they would not have crucified the Lord of glory. But as it is written, 'Things no eye has seen and no ear has heard, that have not entered the heart of mankind— these things God has prepared for those who love Him'" (I Corinthians 2:8-9).*

God saw us as Jesus hung on Calvary's cross, He saw this moment and the moment to come. *1 Corinthians 15:51-57: "Behold, I tell you a mystery: We shall not all sleep, but we shall all be changed—in a moment, in the twinkling of an eye, at the last shofar. For the shofar will sound, and the dead will be raised incorruptible, and we will be changed. For this corruptible must put on incorruptibility, and this mortal must put on immortality. But when this corruptible will have put on incorruptibility and this mortal will have put on immortality, then shall come to pass the saying that is written: 'Death is swallowed up in victory.' 'Where, O Death, is your victory? Where, O Death, is your sting?'"*

Those who have died with the Messiah have first priority on the journey of our final glorious metamorphosis. Scripture says that those who died united with the Messiah will be first. Death was the last enemy to be destroyed. **"The last enemy to be destroyed is death" I Corinthians 15:26 (ESV).** Jesus caused Satan and hell's principalities to make a fool of themselves, so to speak, by stripping their authority and power from the domain of the earth, and Jesus took the dominion and authority over Hell. Likewise, we have authority over the principalities and powers through the blood of Jesus. Ephesians 6:10-18 (NKJV) reveals our spiritual warfare and what armor we must bear to defeat the enemy. *"Finally, my brethren, be strong in the Lord and in the power of His might. Put on the whole armor of God, that you may be able to stand against the wiles of the devil. For we do not wrestle against flesh and blood, but against principalities, against powers, against the rulers of the darkness of this age, against spiritual hosts of wickedness in the heavenly places. Therefore take up the whole armor of God, that you may be able to withstand in the evil day, and having done all, to stand.*

Stand therefore, having girded your waist with truth, having put on the breastplate of righteousness, and having shod your feet with the preparation of the gospel of peace; above all, taking the shield of faith with which you will be able to quench all the fiery darts of the wicked one. And take the helmet of salvation, and the sword of the Spirit, which is the word of God; praying always with all prayer and supplication in the Spirit, being watchful to this end with all perseverance and supplication for all the saints." They still have a spiritual right to function in the second heaven, which is within their realm. But the authority and dominion over the earth were granted back to us because of the blood of Jesus. *"God made you alive together with Him when He pardoned us all our transgressions. He wiped out the handwritten record of debts with the decrees against us, which was hostile to us. He took it away by nailing it to the cross. After disarming the principalities and powers, He made a public spectacle of them, triumphing over them in the cross" (Colossians 2:13-15).*

Satan lost the battle in Heaven, and He lost the battle in Hell. He will ultimately be defeated on earth at the second coming of Christ. However, we are equipped to damage his kingdom and authority in the meantime.

Even though we may be walking around "alive" based on the body's processes, we are nothing more than walking corpses because of the penalty of sin. He didn't decide to wait on man to be "good enough" for Him to die. If They had thought that we could do it independently of Them, there would have been no reason for Him to become flesh and live on earth. We were enemies of God through our sinful natures. Yet, He died for His enemies. What man would do this? How much unconditional and surpassing love is expressed for a man to literally lay down His own life to the point that while suffering, He prayed for His murderers and asked God to forgive them? So often we take for granted this narrative of His death. I urge you to renew your minds by the Spirit to **Romans**

5:7-8: "For while we were still helpless, at the right time Messiah died for the ungodly. For rarely will anyone die for a righteous man—though perhaps for a good man someone might even dare to die. But God demonstrates His own love toward us, in that while we were yet sinners, Messiah died for us."

This forges us on to the place where all of His works created an eternal life for us to enjoy forever and ever. Heaven became our temporary holding place, instead of Sheol, until the New Heaven comes down to earth as previously mentioned. If Paradise in Sheol had satisfied Him, we wouldn't be having this conversation.

Chapter 13

The Grand Final Destination of Heaven

"Heaven is a real place. The more we know about it, the more we should anticipate it. As I have often suggested, Heaven is a prepared place for prepared people." ~ Don Piper

Adam and Eve were removed from the Garden so that they would not reach out their hands and eat from the Tree of Life and live forever in their fallen state, which separated them from having a right relationship with God. However, The Tree of Life didn't get wasted. According to scripture, its leaves are for the healing of the nations. Many testimonies from NDEs have spoken of this huge massive beautiful tree and the fragrance of its leaves and fruits that are unlike anything we have seen or can imagine here on earth.

We will partake of the River of Life and eat from the Tree of Life as described in **Revelation 22:1-3: *"Then the angel showed me a river of the water of life—bright as crystal, flowing from the throne of God and of the Lamb down the middle of the city's street. On either side of the river was a tree of life, bearing twelve kinds of fruit, yielding its fruit each month; and the leaves of the tree were for the healing of the nations. No longer will there be any curse. The throne of God and of the Lamb shall be in the city, and His servants shall serve Him."*** What restoration! Jesus took Eden and brought it to Paradise in the city of God and the

Lamb. This eternal life is what gives hope that no matter what we may be going through, it is nothing compared to what we have to look forward to.

Many have expressed their interest in what Heaven looks like. There have been many confirmations of the description of the Heavenly City in **Revelation 21** from those who have been there. However, let's be ever so careful to acknowledge that the Word of God contains so many answers that pertain to life, death, and everything in-between. But we all have an individual responsibility to search it out for ourselves. We must not be dependent on being spoon-fed by preachers, teachers, evangelists, apostles, prophets. They are to equip and strengthen us, but we are to be responsible for working through our own salvation, and that includes reading His book.

"*And he spoke with me, saying, 'Come, I will show you the bride, the wife of the Lamb.' Then he carried me away in the Ruach to a great and high mountain, and he showed me the holy city, Jerusalem, coming down out of heaven from God, having the glory of God—her radiance like a most precious stone, like a jasper, sparkling like crystal. She had a great, high wall, with twelve gates, and above the gates twelve angels. On the gates were inscribed the names of the twelve tribes of Bnei-Yisrael—three gates on the east, three gates on the north, three gates on the south, and three gates on the west. And the wall of the city had twelve foundations, and on them the twelve names of the twelve emissaries of the Lamb.*

"*The angel speaking with me had a gold measuring rod to measure the city and its gates and walls. The city is laid out as a square—its length the same as its width. He measured the city with the rod—12,000 stadia. Its length and width and height* are equal. He also measured its wall—144 cubits by human measurement, which is also an angel's measurement. The material of the city's wall was jasper, while the city was pure gold, clear as glass. The foundations of the city wall were decorated with every kind of precious stone—the first foundation was jasper; the second, sapphire; the third, chalcedony; the fourth, emerald; the fifth, sardonyx; the sixth, carnelian; the seventh, yellow topaz; the eighth; beryl; the ninth, topaz; the tenth, chrysoprase; the eleventh, jacinth; the twelfth, amethyst. And the twelve gates were twelve pearls—each of the gates was from a single pearl. And the street of the city was pure gold, transparent as glass.

"I saw no temple in her, for its Temple is Adonai Elohei-Tzva'ot and the Lamb. And the city has no need for the sun or the moon to shine on it, for the glory of God lights it up, and its lamp is the Lamb. The nations shall walk by its light, and the kings of the earth bring their glory into it. Its gates shall never be shut by day, for there shall be no night there! And they shall bring into it the glory and honor of the nations. And nothing unholy[n] shall ever enter it, nor anyone doing what is detestable or false, but only those written in the Book of Life."

However, there was a book that I bought after hearing the compelling testimony of Seneca Sodi, occurring over 100 years ago, that chronicled his experience of being in Heaven for 40 days. Mr. Sodi recounts the radiance and splendor of what appeared to be the perfect sunny day. Beautiful greenery, flowers, and trees with aromatic fruits. The area was bustling with happy shining faces of joy and contentment, dressed in white robes in different patterns. The beautiful infrastructure of the winding streets was laid out in a manner that was captivating. He had a feeling of being home.

I don't want anyone to miss this glorious life that Jesus has prepared for those who accepted His plan of salvation. For anyone reading this book, my prayer is that you allow the Holy Spirit to speak to your heart, and if you have never done so, my hope is that you will accept Him as YOUR Lord and Savior. ***"Saving us is the greatest and most concrete demonstration of God's love, the definitive display of His grace throughout time and eternity." ~David Jeremiah.***

How fundamental is **Matthew 25** to understanding the predominance to God that we love and take care of one another? This has been the repeated utterance from countless NDEers: love is the key to everything. The simplicity of love and bestowing kindness on others should be done as if we are doing them for Him. Being in His presence overshadows everything. ***"You make known to me the path of life. Abundance of joys are in Your presence, eternal pleasures at Your right hand" (Psalm 16:11).***

The Church loves to bellow about our mansions of glory in Heaven. ***Enoch 41:1-2: "And after that I saw all the secrets of the heavens, and how the kingdom is divided, and how the actions of men are weighed in the balance. And there I saw the mansions of the elect and the mansions of the holy."*** Otherwise, the King James Version translated *rooms* for *mansions* in **John 14.** But it doesn't matter because our earthly ideas will never be accurate to what Jesus' idea of what a room or mansion is. He does superiorly more than we can think. When we consider the work of His hands through the creation, how much more brilliant would the work of His hands be for our next transition into eternal life?

The Holy Spirit helped me to understand through what He spoke to me about Uncle's transition; although someone may make it to Heaven because of salvation, there are different levels of rewards in Heaven, and the degrees or levels are based on what we did on earth. The more you serve the Lord, the faster you get to arrive at the Throne of God in the Holy City versus residing in Paradise, which lies in the suburbs of Heaven. Salvation is not based on works; it is based on the blood of Jesus and accepting His finished work of Christ as the Son of God. *"For by grace you have been saved through faith. And this is not from yourselves—it is the gift of God. It is not based on deeds, so that no one may boast. For we are His workmanship—created in Messiah Yeshua for good deeds, which God prepared beforehand so we might walk in them" (Ephesians 2:8-10).* So, let's examine the word of God about this matter.

Firstly, it is clear, according to **I Corinthians 3:12-17,** that God has a systematic way of determining the quality of our works. Therefore, it is not necessarily the quantity of our deeds but the quality, and not just the quality but the motive of the heart. Are the deeds done out of a pure heart, or to be seen and feel prideful in the eyes of man?

1 Corinthians 3:12-17: "Now if anyone builds on the foundation with gold, silver, precious stones, wood, hay, straw, each one's work will become clear. For the Day will show it, because it is to be revealed by fire; and the fire itself will test each one's work—what sort it is. If anyone's work built on the foundation survives, he will receive a reward. If anyone's work is burned up, he will suffer loss—he himself will be saved, but as through fire."

So, I began to inquire of the Lord about achieving the balance of not trying to do works just to get a reward in heaven. *"The heart and motive is the key to it all,"* He said. *"For this is precisely what I warned the religious men of My day against. Go look in My Word and remind yourself of what I said."* So, I intently looked at **Matthew 6:1-6** again and again, until the words penetrated my spirit through and through.

"Be careful not to practice your righteousness in front of others to be seen by them. If you do, you will have no reward from your Father in heaven. So when you give to the needy, do not announce it with trumpets, as the hypocrites do in the synagogues and on the streets, to be honored by others. Truly I tell you, they have received their reward in full. But when you give to the needy, do not let your left hand know what your right hand is doing, so that your giving may be in secret. Then your Father, who sees what is done in secret, will reward you. And when you pray, do not be like the hypocrites, for they love to pray standing in the synagogues and on the street corners to be seen by others. Truly I tell you, they have received their reward in full. But when you pray, go into your room, close the door and pray to your Father, who is unseen. Then your Father, who sees what is done in secret, will reward you" (NIV).

"When you fast, do not look somber as the hypocrites do, for they disfigure their faces to show others they are fasting. Truly I tell you, they have received their reward in full. But when you fast, put oil on your head and wash your face, so that it will not be obvious to others that you are fasting, but only to your Father, who is unseen; and your Father, who sees what is done in secret, will reward you" Matthew 6:16-18 (NIV).

There is no other clearer illustration than this narrative of performing "works" of God to be seen and elevated in man's eyes, instead of doing them from a heart of love and humility for the Lord. They are to be done for Him regardless of who sees or knows what you are doing. The accolades that man will reward are fleeting, but the accolades and rewards that God bestows upon us are greater and will be granted in eternal life. So, don't worry about whether your legacy is seen and known by society or man, because what you do in secret, God will reward you openly. That's the legacy to strive for.

Yet, **Matthew 20** has been deemed as unfair and often used to justify that we all are rewarded equally the same. The latter is true in the sense of salvation. Whether we have been saved for 99 years or 99 seconds, there's the denarius of salvation that is paid equally. Salvation can't be bought, purchased, or obtained through any measure of good deeds.

In essence, in the parable, the landowner, who represented Jesus, had workers who started their labor at different times, but in the end, they were paid the same wage, but the ones that started the latest got paid first. The workers were disgruntled by the landowner's methods. Nonetheless, He challenges them by asserting that He has the right to do as He pleases with what is His. He also affirms that He is generous. Jesus is generous with His grace and mercy. His life was far more precious than a denarius. To drive this home, let's break it down into a more relatable example. The thief that died beside Jesus, who was told that today, you will be with Me in Paradise, received the same reward of salvation as the disciples who were with Jesus from the beginning of His ministry. When we step back and contend with the scripture from that vantage point, it doesn't appear fair at all. But it reveals the heart of the Savior. Hallelujah!

"For the kingdom of heaven is like a landowner who went out early in the morning to hire workers for his vineyard. He agreed to pay them a denarius for the day and sent them into his vineyard. About nine in the morning he went out and saw others

standing in the marketplace doing nothing. He told them, 'You also go and work in my vineyard, and I will pay you whatever is right.' So they went. He went out again about noon and about three in the afternoon and did the same thing. About five in the afternoon he went out and found still others standing around. He asked them, 'Why have you been standing here all day long doing nothing?' 'Because no one has hired us,' they answered. He said to them, 'You also go and work in my vineyard.' When evening came, the owner of the vineyard said to his foreman, 'Call the workers and pay them their wages, beginning with the last ones hired and going on to the first.' The workers who were hired about five in the afternoon came and each received a denarius. So when those came who were hired first, they expected to receive more. But each one of them also received a denarius. When they received it, they began to grumble against the landowner. 'These who were hired last worked only one hour,' they said, 'and you have made them equal to us who have borne the burden of the work and the heat of the day.' But he answered one of them, 'I am not being unfair to you, friend. Didn't you agree to work for a denarius? Take your pay and go. I want to give the one who was hired last the same as I gave you. Don't I have the right to do what I want with my own money? Or are you envious because I am generous?' So the last will be first, and the first will be last" (Matthew 20:1-16).

We must appreciate the new commandment that Jesus left us with: **"*I give you a new commandment, that you love one another. Just as I have loved you, so also you must love one another. By this all will know that you are My disciples, if you have love for one another" (John 13:34).*** To understand the legacy of love, let's review **Matthew 25:31-46:**

"Now when the Son of Man comes in His glory, and all the angels with Him, then He will sit on His glorious throne. All the nations will be gathered before Him, and He will separate them from one another, just as the shepherd separates the sheep from the goats. And He will put the sheep on His right, but the goats on His left. Then the King will say to those on His right, 'Come, you who are blessed by My Father, inherit the kingdom prepared for you from the foundation of the world. For I was hungry and you gave Me something to eat; I was thirsty and you gave Me something to drink; I was a stranger and you invited Me in; I was naked and you clothed Me; I was sick and you visited Me; I was in prison and you came to Me.' Then the righteous will answer Him, 'Lord, when did we see You hungry and feed You? Or thirsty and give You something to drink? And when did we see You a stranger and invite You in? Or naked and clothe You? When did we see You sick, or in prison, and come to You?' And answering, the King will say to them, 'Amen, I tell you, whatever you did to one of the least of these My brethren, you did it to Me.' Then He will also say to those on the left, 'Go away from Me, you cursed ones, into the everlasting fire which has been prepared for the devil and his angels. For I was hungry and you gave Me nothing to eat; I was thirsty and you gave Me nothing to drink; I was a stranger and you did not invite Me in; naked and you did not clothe Me; sick and in prison and you did not visit Me.' Then they too will answer, saying, 'Lord, when did we see You hungry or thirsty or a stranger or naked or sick or in prison, and did not care for You?' Then He will answer them, saying, 'Amen, I tell you, whatever you did not do for one of the least of these, you did not do for Me.' These shall go off to everlasting punishment, but the righteous into everlasting life."

We see these acts of love and kindness doesn't seem that big of a deal in the grand scheme of things to do for the Lord. Yet, He takes them very seriously, but not just seriously but personally, as it reflects the care and concern for our brothers and sisters. I shrink and shudder at the thought of churches who wouldn't help pay someone's light bill and leave them in the dark and cold but will pay thousands of dollars to have a well-known musical artist or speaker to teach or preach at a church conference. Many well-known preachers and evangelists require their plane tickets to be paid and even five-star hotel accommodations in addition to paying them for their "services." I recall a friend of mine who was very upset and ashamed that during their church meeting, their benevolence cost for the whole year was $1,200. But the cost for entertainment paid for Christian music artists and guest speakers was $135,000. That ought not to be. We are sternly warned in **Matthew 7:21-23** the consequences of these types of actions. This is all connected. These spiritual acts of the Church do NOT supersede the common acts of brotherly love. *"Not everyone who says to Me, 'Lord, Lord!' will enter the kingdom of heaven, but he who does the will of My Father in heaven. Many will say to Me on that day, 'Lord, Lord, didn't we prophesy in Your name, and drive out demons in Your name, and perform many miracles in Your name?' Then I will declare to them, 'I never knew you. Get away from Me, you workers of lawlessness!'"* Jesus never demonstrated a tolerance of religious piety and false righteousness of men. He certainly demonstrated this toward the Pharisees and Sadducees of His day and certainly alluded to the same in this scripture.

Romans 2:5-11 similarly speaks of rewards based on the condition of the heart in terms of attitude. *"But by your hard and unrepentant heart, you are storing up wrath for yourself on the* *day of wrath, when God's righteous judgment is revealed. He will pay back each person according to his deeds. To those who by perseverance in doing good are seeking glory, honor, and immortality—eternal life. But to those who are self-seeking and do not obey the truth, but obey unrighteousness—wrath and fury. There will be trouble and hardship for every human soul that does evil—to the Jew first and also to the Greek. But there will be glory, honor, and shalom to everyone who does good—to the Jew first and also to the Greek. For there is no partiality with God."*

The heart of the matter, no pun intended, is this: Jews and Greek were under the same venture to accept the truth of Yeshua, the Messiah, who was the Son of God, crucified, and raised from the dead. Now keep in mind that the religious leaders engaged in a coverup to conceal the resurrection. Despite all of the religious and pious dogma of the pompous religious men of Jesus' time, the legacy they left bore a false witness against the most miraculous event that had ever occurred. Consequently, instead of softening their hearts, repenting, and believing in Him, they choose to pay off the guards and spread the false narrative, that is still said to this very day, that the disciples stole His body. *"While the women were on their way, some of the guards went into the city and reported to the chief priests everything that had happened. When the chief priests had met with the elders and devised a plan, they gave the soldiers a large sum of money, telling them, 'You are to say, "His disciples came during the night and stole him away while we were asleep." If this report gets to the governor, we will satisfy him and keep you out of trouble.' So the soldiers took the money and did as they were instructed. And this story has been widely circulated among the Jews to this very day"* (Matthew 28:11-15).

I find nothing more compelling to complete this summation than the words and experience of Seneca Sodi's time in Heaven. He describes one of the events in Heaven of witnessing a new arrival to Paradise. She seemed unsure and confused as to why she was in Heaven, being that she didn't feel worthy to be there, based on her earthly life. She was taking it all in as she was seeing the purest white garments, the Tree of Life, and the golden cups. She felt this was surely a mistake, as she confessed how she had been a great sinner, with which the angel agreed. But the attendant reassured her that the angels cannot make a mistake and that she was saved, but as one snatched from the fire. With an earnest and tender heart, they reminded her that she did not make good use of her salvation and wasn't faithful to God. Therefore, she couldn't be rewarded because she did not build with gold, silver, and precious stones, but with wood, hay and stubble, which have been burnt. God was unable to reward her with anything other than her salvation and forgiveness of her sins.

Therefore, she was not given a wedding garment, but just a simple white robe. However, the elder explained that she would have to make advancements in Paradise that should have been accomplished on earth. But she would be assisted in gaining more knowledge about Christ and His salvation. Seneca Sodi inquired of the elder for clarification of what was taking place with this situation. The elder explained that she represents a large portion of Christians, who get saved, but never really grow or mature in their salvation. They do not produce any treasure in Heaven and their soul feels that great loss. However, they must reside in Paradise, which is on the outside, surrounding the Holy City, where the throne of God abides. But even Paradise bears more glory than they ever feel they deserve. But God is great in His mercy and lovingkindness towards us. The leaves on the Tree are for the healing of the nations, and she will partake of that tree and be healed.

Even if you are skeptical of the written experiences of Seneca Sodi, please take note that what he describes is scriptural through and through. This is a clear portrait of being saved but having not laid up any treasure in Heaven and feeling the loss of that. **Matthew 25:14-28** illustrates the different measures of our abilities to work for the Lord. *"Again, it will be like a man going on a journey, who called his servants and entrusted his wealth to them. To one he gave five bags of gold, to another two bags, and to another one bag, each according to his ability."*

God always will equip us with what we need to complete our destiny in Him. The more that He gives us, the more responsible we are for our actions. Therefore, the more life and ways of God that we have inside of us and the more that we know Him and His ways, the more will be required of us.

"That slave who knew his master's will but did not prepare or act according to his desire will be harshly whipped. But the one who did not know and did things worthy of a beating will be whipped lightly. From everyone given much, much will be required; and from the one for whom more is provided, all the more they will ask of him" (Luke 12:47-48).

Speaking of slaves, from an earthly standpoint of black slavery in America, Seneca Sodi referred to race, prejudice, and evil masters who appeared holy on Sunday and cruel the other six days to his family and his slaves. The master didn't make it to Heaven. Seneca Sodi's mother pointed out to him that there was no racism or prejudice in Heaven. Seneca clarified if she was saying there were no different distinct races. His mother stated that there are distinct races but no prejudice based on race. But that all is one big Heavenly family regardless of what the color of their body was on earth. But then she noted a group of souls singing and she told her son that those were American slaves who had suffered much while on earth from their harsh masters. Seneca recognized one of them, named Rastus, who was one of the slaves on the ship that Seneca had preached to. Seneca asked if Rastus' master was there, and he stated that he had never seen him in the Heavenly domain. He recalls how his master acted good in public on Sunday but was cruel to his family and slaves the other six days. Rastus was overjoyed by all that was his in Heaven after being so poor and mistreated while on earth.

Our salvation is the conduit that gives us the right to enter into Heaven. However, the measure of our treasures in Heaven is completely predicated by us.

Chapter 14

The Fingerprints of Transition

"I've always believed there are moments in our lives which can be defined as a transition between the before and after, between the cause and the effect." ~ Benjamin X. Wretlind

Transition is defined as a process or a period of changing from one state or condition to another. Therefore, there are transitioning processes in life and death, physically and spiritually. The transition involving childbirth involves both physical and psychological changes in our human bodies. The most intense phase, where the cervix goes from 8 cm to full dilation, is known as the transition phase. The body is right at the brink of delivering a new life. The contractions become longer, stronger, and more intense. This is the phase that many mockeries of a mother growling and cursing her spouse are derived from. The best thing is, it's typically the shortest period of the labor process. But one principle that holds true is, "For every reaction, there is an equal and opposite reaction." So, if there is a transition that occurs with bringing life into the world, then there's certainly one that occurs with the end of life, although the differences in the transition processes are not similar. Transition in death is far more dramatic and alluring than that of childbirth.

There are physical and psychological characteristics that point to an expected time frame of impending death. As a hospice nurse,

I was trained on how to recognize these physical and psychological signs and educated the caregivers on how to recognize them as well. This allowed the family to have some sense of preparation, although there is nothing that can fully prepare anyone for the finality of a loved one's last breath. One of the most distinctive aspects of the transition process at the end-of-life is the detachment from the people in this world. The person begins to withdraw from this life and stops talking and interacting with their loved ones. It is described as going inside of themselves. The detachment often occurs first with the person that is closest to them, such as a spouse, child, or mother. It is painful to see that a loved one's body is still here, yet all forms of interaction and conversation cease a few days or weeks before earthly life completely subsides. This is very difficult for family and friends to understand, and many times they take it personally. The feeling of rejection or thinking their loved one was upset or angry with them may add to their grief. But this is a part of the dying loved one's "letting go" and acceptance that life on this side is ending. It is crucial for the grieving loved one to understand this.

This is often the time that the dying one may see and/or talk to deceased loved ones, speak of angels or demons, heaven or hell. We often say that they are hallucinating, but are they? When there is one foot in the earthly present and one foot in the spiritual afterlife, these "hallucinations" may be genuine visions and experiences. I have witnessed countless patients have these experiences.

I have greatly anticipated sharing the incredible experiences that the Lord granted me surrounding my son's transition from his earthly life into his eternal life in Paradise. At one point, I would have said that nothing could have prepared me for what I have been through with the death of my sweet boy. But I can assure you

The Fingerprints of Transition

that God did everything to literally prepare me, just shy of directly telling me when it was going to happen.

Along this painful journey, I have been able to see the beautiful handwriting on the wall by a loving Father and Friend, who did prepare me along the way. Looking through the needle hole of our grief and pain from the death of a loved one, we often are not able to see the complete picture of His preparation. But as we turn our pain into trusting that He promised to give beauty for ashes, gladness for mourning, and peace for despair, regardless of the situation, we can activate the faith that starts the healing process by His strength. The definition of *in-between* is an adjective that means "situated between two extremes or recognized categories."

There was a professional and personal understanding about the transition processes in life with childbirth and in the dying of the terminally ill, but now, here lies a new and relatively personal territory to explore, which unveiled itself after I lost my son.

There is a notable transition between life and death of a loved one who is going to pass away from this earth suddenly, which is quite different from when we have some sort of expectation with the terminally ill. The fingerprints of transition are smeared on the mirror of our souls and are seemingly undetected until after a death, especially a sudden, unexpected death. During terminal illness, there's some measure of preparation; however, with the sudden or unexpected death, there's not a shred of preparation on a conscious level. The reflection of events, things said, things done, a feeling, a dream, etc., involving your loved one who has passed away can be rather startling. Even the smallest details can connect the dots on the trajectory to impending life after life. For example, the day before my uncle died, while attending a cookout graduation celebration for my niece, he was talking a great deal about his mother, who had been deceased for many years. This was unusual for him to talk about her so extensively. Another account involved a close family friend who lost her twelve-year-old son in a tragic car accident. But shortly before this event, they had a wonderful healing in their relationship. I could go on and on about acts of transition. Later, I will go into greater detail about my transitioning experiences with my son.

Nonetheless, the short synopses of these experiences are more than mere coincidences or fleeting happenstance. I'm sure that if you took a few minutes of silence to reflect on your own loss of a loved one, you would be able to identify a similar moment or experience. There have been countless stories of people recalling circumstances, much like these that occurred before their loved one transitioned. Other times there was something good that has happened or a change that had occurred in that person's life just shortly before they crossed over. ***Ecclesiastes 7:8*** outlines the essence of transitioning in-between life and death in this manner: ***"Better the end of a matter than its beginning."***

One lady, whom I will call Nancy, recently recounted to me losing her 34-year-old son in a tragic motorcycle accident where the bike caught on fire. But what made it more painful for her was her recollection on how he had finally achieved some good things in his life that she described as being in the best place of his life that he'd ever been in with his job and fiancée. She expressed how unfair it was for his life to be cut off at that time. She even felt anger towards God whom she had been serving and living for until "He took my son!" as she exclaimed. As we touched on this matter in the previous chapters, this is a common reaction to loss. She echoed the same belief that many do. My heart broke by knowing firsthand the pain of her loss, and yet, knowing that the very God she shunned was the only One who could help her through this difficult time. It saddens me that God is the most misunderstood person on the planet.

As she was recounting the story to me, I began to ponder this enigma of something good happening or a happy moment before death occurs. Even as a nurse, there's a common saying of, "they get better before they get worse." It is a known phenomenon that someone will have a really great day and appear to have been making a full recovery right before they die. Then the Teacher and Bearer of All Truth solidified Ecclesiastes 7:8 to me: *"That's it, Lord! I see!"* I said. Although He gets blamed for the act of death, He is not offended or put off by our accusations because nothing can separate us from His love. ***"For I am convinced that neither death nor life, nor angels nor principalities, nor things present nor things to come, nor powers, nor height nor depth, nor any other created thing will be able to separate us from the love of God that is in Messiah Yeshua our Lord"*** *(Romans 8:38-39).*

Within the confines of His love for the one departing and those who remain, He grants a crescendo at the final curtain call of this life. A pivotal moment occurs to give the survivor(s) a good memory that's clothed in peace. Yet, the enemy of our soul misapplies these moments and causes sorrow with thoughts of how unfair it is for them to die now when everything was seemingly "good" for them. It bears witness that for the departing one themselves, there is joy or light that transcends their natural existence. Just like a light bulb that gives out a big burst of light right before it dies out, such is the close timing of death in the life of a child of God. This brightness or renewal of what is about to take place spiritually in death can sometimes be seen physically. However, it is not evident to the natural mind that this is what is occurring until after the cessation of earthly living. Then, it clicks. You can look back at a picture they had just taken or how they seemed to appear the last time you saw them. This is precisely what mirrored my son's transcendence of light, joy, and love, as evident by a glow that could be seen and felt from his photos taken the day before he transitioned out of this life.

Recently, I watched a documentary about the Emanuel AME Church shooting in 2015. One of the victims' husband recounted that there was a glow and happiness about his wife that he just couldn't explain. He said she was singing and he felt he could actually see a glow around her. He stated that he had a thought of going over to hug her and as he did, it was as if something stopped him and said, "Don't touch her." He said that now he knows she had already transitioned to the heavenly realm, as she was shortly shot to death while attending bible study. Wow! That gives me chills from head to toe every time I reflect on that story, mostly because I understand it. It bears witness with me in a way that is beyond comprehension.

Transitioning serves as a beacon of light God gave us to help guide us through His process of the interchange between life and death. What is unseen is the key to it all. God's motif is truly a bestowal of grandeur for us when we have our spiritual marching orders towards eternity.

My personal experience with transitioning between life and death has been incredibly sobering to recall how everything was coming into alignment for the graduation from this life for my sweet boy. The full transition process occurred over six months from November 2015 to May 2016.

Starting in September 2015, I began to have an unsettling burden to pray for my son to move from California. I had a deep and troubling premonition that something bad was going to

The Fingerprints of Transition

happen. I wasn't sure if it was going to happen involving the state of California or specifically him, but I bore a deep intense foreboding that my son needed to leave from there as soon as possible. This was not some whimsical desire as a mother that felt she was too far from her son. It was a deep, compelling urgency as if I were racing against time, only to now understand that it truly was. My son loved California, so I was expecting some intense debate to turn his heart and mind to leave and come to Alabama, where his sisters and I resided. But God moved the circumstances like a pawn on a chessboard, and before I knew it, he was flying to Nashville for me to pick him up. The first step into his transition phase had been taken.

He arrived home extremely broken and discouraged with life. Frankly, he was mad at God after reeling from the pain of his girlfriend's sudden and unexpected death. Incredibly, just like I expected, over the next four months, he began to make some great leaps in his journey of healing. Nonetheless, I knew his heart was now etched with a deep scar.

He spent some great quality time with me, his five sisters, his nephew, and his nieces. The love of his family was The Chicken Soup for his soul. He had enrolled in and started a truck driving program. Due to his training, he was going to be traveling on the road for several months after he completed his classroom curriculum. He felt a strong need to travel to our hometown in Tennessee to visit with family and friends. He had spent time with so many people during the last three months of his life. He actually had a mental list of people that he wanted to see. This was quite amazing, as if his spirit knew that he was about to take flight and was saying his last goodbyes.

Most significantly, he spent his 27th birthday with his dad.

This doesn't seem that important unless I explain.

He had a lot of struggles with his relationship with his dad. We always talked openly and honestly about the importance of forgiveness. I would encourage him to focus specifically on forgiving his dad. In times past, he would shrug it off with a negative reply. I don't know when it happened, but something incredible happened in his heart towards his dad a month before he died. The healing with his dad was divinely a result of the Holy Spirit's mighty hand, and that healing was rock solid. Forgiveness is one of the most pivotal things that God demands of us. Love and forgiveness are His law. ***Matthew 6:14-15 ESV: "For if you forgive others their trespasses, your heavenly Father will also forgive you. But if you do not forgive others their trespasses, neither will your Father forgive your trespasses."*** This is also part of the Lord's Prayer. Without forgiveness, our sins cannot be pardoned; therefore, we will not be in right fellowship with God. We can bust down the doors of the church every Wednesday and Sunday, but a heart of unforgiveness will block that relationship with the Father because although He died on the cross for our sins, He can't forgive them unless we also forgive others. That really puts a big responsibility on us to do our part in our relationship with the Lord.

My son had made steps towards building a relationship with his father, and that brought so much joy to my heart. I will never forget the words when he said to me, "Oh, I've gotten over all of that stuff. I don't hold anything against him." Wow! What? Really!? It's hard to articulate how intense this was, and upon reflection, it still is.

We engaged in passionate spiritual conversations about many aspects of life. Forgiveness was one of the main topics. As I contemplated the events of those last months with him, I recall

The Fingerprints of Transition

two very awe-filled conversations about death. Most paramount was our conversation regarding what happens when we die. He said, "But how does anyone know what happens after we die?" I explained the biblical account of Lazarus and the rich man in Luke 16:25-31, which explains several aspects of death, as we expounded on previously. I continued to explain to him that God was allowing us to know more details about death, Heaven, and Hell in our modern times through thousands of accounts of people's near-death experiences. I had a DVD called *Beyond the Grave*, which described individuals' accounts of seeing Heaven and Hell. I was memorized by the stories of the individuals. This video jumpstarted my interest in learning more about these gifts that God has allowed us to learn from. Moving on, just like the urgency to pray for him to move from California, was that same pressing urgency to have him watch that DVD and believe what I was telling him. I couldn't explain or understand why I felt so strongly that I needed him to believe and understand that death was not the end. This is spine-chilling now that he is gone because it's like I had a subliminal message trying to prepare him for what was about to occur, although he professed not to have any fear of death.

During our second penetrating conversation, words like *prophetic*, *premonition*, and *foreboding* come to mind. As we were discussing death, he forcefully expressed that he hoped to die before me because he wouldn't be able to deal with me passing away. Of course, this caused immense sorrow at just the mere thought of him passing away. Actually, it was virtually impossible to bring such an atrocity to my psyche. Filled with exasperation and torment, I uttered that no parent wants to bury their child and that he couldn't possibly imagine how painful that would be for me! We ended that conversation with my heart feeling like that large rainbow elephant in the room bore down its two-ton body and crushed my chest! Grievously, this time, it was as if he were trying to prepare me for what was about to occur. For this hypothetical situation had now become the pervasive reality that he hoped for.

The Lord, in His mercy and grace, allowed my son to experience many great moments shortly before he stepped into eternity, and his life was in the best place that he had been in a long time as an adult. We were able to celebrate Christmas, New Years, and my birthday with him. The last bliss for him was attending his best friend's wedding as his best man, the last greatest moment of his life. He died the next morning.

God did not cause my son to die. Yet, because He knew exactly when he would, I can envision His sketch drawing, like an old pirate treasure map, of the events that He did plan to make that horrific moment, as we received the news, more supportable for us.

The weekend that he passed, God allowed me and four of my girls to be in Tennessee all at the same time, which was highly unusual. This allowed us to be with our extended family for the support that we all needed. Paul Brian died in Atlanta, GA, instead of California or somewhere else in the United States like Utah. He had started a new job as a truck driver and was driving all across the nation. He had been in Utah several times a month and even as far as New Mexico. God, in His bountiful love, knew how much harder and more disastrous things could have been, such as him lying dead for days or weeks in a truck or hotel room before anyone found him, or being thousands of miles away and having to make arrangements to go identify him and retain his body. As horrific as it was getting the phone call that my son had passed, it could have been so much more lamentable under these circumstances. His countenance in his last photos the day before he passed away,

The Fingerprints of Transition

resonated a renewed brightness on his face that shone bright like a diamond. He looked free and whole.

Were all of these things mere coincidences? Absolutely not! They were the fingerprints of God's doing. God knows things that we do not know. His transition from life, death, and everything in-between was orchestrated with grace and mercy by a wise heavenly Father. For me, his mother, these parts of his transition are unremitting in my mind. ***"Life is pleasant. Death is peaceful. It's the transition that's troublesome." Isaac Asimov.***

Those were natural earthly parts of the transition that occurred, but another part of the transition occurred about one year before my son's death. With one audacious cruel onslaught of reality, the recesses of my soul went off like a bolt of lightning. I was partially warned of this moment. I had a very vivid dream that I was delivering a eulogy at Central Baptist Church in Kingsport, TN. I saw everything in the dream except for whose eulogy it was. However, I could recall every lifelike detail of the dream. I never forgot one shred of detail.

I saw the closed casket positioned in the front of the church. I saw the dress I was wearing. I recalled that the church was very crowded. It was so profoundly real that I jumped up that morning and said matter-of-factly to my youngest daughter, *"I don't know who it was, but I'm going to be delivering a eulogy at Central Baptist Church one day."* It was just that simple and factual to me. Honestly, I thought that it would be for my dad, who was suffering from dementia. ***Corinthians 13:9 NIV*** reminds us that ***"Now our knowledge is partial and incomplete, and even the gift of prophecy reveals only part of the whole picture!"*** The Lord knew that I could only handle the partial knowledge that concealed the identity of whose shell was lying there in that casket. After I came to this astounding realization, it never occurred to me how I was going to be able to do it. I just knew that I had to. It felt very natural that I should be the one to deliver his eulogy to sign off on his death, just like I had to sign his birth certificate to sign off on his birth.

I did so with and by the power of the Holy Spirit. Honestly, if someone had ever asked me before this, if I could deliver a eulogy for any of my children, I would have been mortified by that thought! But God had prepared me, in the vastness of my soul, to carry out the vision by equipping me with strength beyond comprehension at the moment He opened up the dream or vision to me a year before I was set to fulfill it.

This was actually a very defining moment because I completely overcame my intense fear of public speaking. I tried to write the words and prepare the eulogy, but it seemed that the words couldn't seem to materialize on paper. So as God would have it, I delivered it impromptu.

The premise of the message was based on Luke 23, the thief on the cross. ***"If you just had a little life left in you and you called on the name of Jesus, He would receive you."*** My mother and others in the crowd told me that when I started speaking about this, the sun suddenly beamed brightly in on me through the church window. I didn't realize it, but it obviously caught the attention of the onlookers. I like to believe that God was winking and smiling at me for sustaining a heart of obedience in the most difficult time of my life and was well pleased.

These experiences echoed the sound truth that God is intentional in how He will hide us under His wings to protect us during the crushing blows of life. Notice that I didn't say that He protects us "from" the crushing blows of life. He already warned that we will have many tests and trials in this life. He left us the tools to use to plant ourselves deep roots of faith and gave us the authority to overcome the world because He overcame the world. *"These things I have spoken to you, so that in Me you may have shalom (peace). In the world you will have trouble, but take heart! I have overcome the world!" (John 16:33).*

I am truly filled with gratitude to the Father for being a bridge over troubled waters when the tears were being poured out like an ocean that was tossing me to and fro with unrelenting pain. Although these transitional moments were impressionable, they are nothing compared to the magnificent spiritual experiences that occurred as part of the greatest signs that foretold of his soon-approaching transition.

Chapter 15

Angelic Visitation

"Numerous have been the manifestations of God's providence in sustaining us. In the gloomy period of adversity, we have had 'our cloud by day and pillar of fire by night.' We have been reduced to distress, and the arm of Omnipotence has raised us up." ~ Samuel Adams.

As previously alluded to, my son was overly excited to attend his best friend, Coty's, wedding on May 28, 2016. On Friday, May 27, 2016, my son had contacted me to make arrangements to bring his tuxedo to Atlanta, GA, for the wedding the next day. Although I was sensing a bit of stress, without warning, an anxious feeling suddenly swept through me as I settled my plans to drive down from Huntsville, AL to Atlanta, GA after work that evening to ensure he had his tuxedo in time. However, to my overwhelming surprise, I heard the most audible reverberating voice that sent shock waves through my whole being. There was a stern but not angry, rebuke with the words, "No, don't go!" This made the very hairs on the back of my neck stand straight up. It still does, as I relive that memory.

I nervously called my son to inform him that I had a change of plans and would bring the tuxedo the next day since there would be ample time before the wedding started that evening. Despite having a sound plan, I couldn't disarm the bone-chilling foreboding that had occurred earlier. As the evening moved on, this turned more into an apprehension that started affecting my whole physical body. I wanted to ask the Lord what was the meaning behind this. But I was partly afraid of what His answer may be. Could I really handle it if it was something that I didn't want to know? I finally succumbed to my own resolve that perhaps the Lord was saving me from a car accident or some other type of tragedy; after all, what else could it have been that warrants an audible voice of warning from God? I didn't tell my best friend or daughter, who were traveling with me, for concern that they may become fearful.

While still discomfited, I attempted to go to bed early to prepare for my trip, but I was deeply troubled in my innermost being; therefore, I was unable to relax and fall into a sound sleep. The endless tossing and turning became overbearing, which led me to get up around 3:00 a.m.

I went into the living room and opened up my laptop to attempt to work on a project for my marketing position, to get my mind off the apprehension that wouldn't take its grip off me. These attempts to remain distracted became utterly futile.

In the stillness of the dark sky, there was a presence looming in the night air that was thick and palpable. Be that as it may, as if someone or something heard my suspicious thoughts, that presence seemed to have coursed through the thick night air and broke through the veil of earth's dimension.

As I sat with my head down, out of my peripheral vision, a flickering light caught my attention. I raised my head to get a full view out the large bay window. It was not a meager flicker of light but a flame of fire highlighting the night sky. I was astonished! The flame was moving at a rapid pace back and forth as if an Olympian were running with the Olympic torch through the middle of the neighbor's backyard. Entertaining my inner dialogue, I asked myself, "Why does the neighbor have a torch in the middle of the night?" As I heard how ludicrous that sounded in my own hearing, I offered my own rebuttal as I said, "People don't use torches anymore." I have no explanation of why a torch was the first thought that came to mind. Perhaps it was the floating motion of the fire that appeared suspended in the air, and in my mind's eye, I pictured someone holding something in their hand that could carry the flame in that manner.

After the inability to satisfy myself with a logical answer, I dismissed it all and lowered my head back down to shift the attention back to my work project. However, it appeared that the more effort that I exerted towards dismantling the thoughts of the flame outside my back window, the more it personified as something not to be ignored. The notion to refute my disruptive intellect became ineffectual.

Just as quickly as this moment began, it quickly escalated to the brink of miraculous. I started to intuitively know that there was a source connected to that flame, but it was indeed not the elderly neighbor next door, so then, who? Or better yet, what was it? With every succession of questioning, the answers immediately presented a little more clarification, seemingly at the speed of thought.

I perceived that something was beckoning me and desired my attention to acknowledge that the flame was significant. Now, this surely sounds like a sci-fi movie or Twilight Zone episode, and I was the main star. My heart began to percolate in the depths of my soul as I was being spurred on again by the soft, yet audible, words: "Look up! Look up!" So, I took a deep breath to entertain what I thought was my imagination and raised my head to look out the window. Now understand that I never lost sight of the flame out of the corner of my eye, but as I looked up, what I saw paralyzed me with overwhelming confusion and astonishment.

My natural eyes had shedded their earthly scales that confine them to this earthly dimension that conceals the spiritual one; however, I was about to see just how much they are existing simultaneously together. Suddenly, I was visualizing something that I immediately perceived as being from the spiritual realm, and it was standing here on earth and right outside my window amid the large trees. I rubbed my eyes and shook my head side to side just to make sure that I wasn't dreaming. Convinced that I was not, with the next look, I beheld the presence of the spiritual being.

The being was suspended in the air but low to the ground without touching it. It was in spirit form; thus, there were no physical legs of flesh to stand upon. We are used to speaking in proximity of things in terms of the body and what is "normal" for Earth. But when it comes to the spiritual realm, it becomes a challenge to find adequate words to describe accurately what was seen or felt. I will reference the being as "he" because I perceived that it was masculine in nature, although the face wasn't clearly visible with the distinct features of a man. His appearance was a transparent, opaque coloration, like a misty cloud that I could see through, but yet solid at the same time. He had a large, strong silhouette. He didn't have wings. In proximity to the tall trees, I would estimate that his stature was approximately 10 -12 feet tall. I did not identify what area of his personage the flame was emanating from. The angel had a militaristic stance, like an English palace guard, but yet exuded a communion of love, care, warmth, compassion, and, most of all, protection. I did take note that the flame was no longer moving back and forth but was completely still, just as he was.

I locked my eyes with a fixed gaze on him, and I trembled at the thought of him speaking to me. But once again, my inner dialogue surfaced, and I began asking, "What do you want? What do you want to tell me?" Instantaneously, as if my words and thoughts were heard, I was granted spiritual knowledge, much like mental telepathy, that he was there on a specific assignment to keep watch over me. I understood that he had not been instructed to give me any kind of message or reveal to me the specific reason for the manifestation. Regardless of the purpose, I trusted God's reason for revealing His Heavenly Messenger, but I knew by the Spirit that it was not good. Perhaps it had something to do with the commanding voice to avoid traveling to Atlanta on Friday evening and the restless uneasiness that had prevented me from sleeping that night. Nonetheless, I knew he was there to take care of me. However, I had no idea how enormous the need for that care would become in the next 24 hours of my life and beyond, but God did.

I remained there in my living room transfixed and gazing out the window until daybreak, at which time he faded from my sight, but I could still sense his presence. Although this left me unwrought, I was comforted at the same time because I felt enormously loved and protected by God, who allowed His ministering spirit to be revealed to me. God wanted to make sure that I would know that no matter what was about to happen, He truly was never going to leave me nor forsake me, just as His word promised.

When events happen with the supernatural, it is human nature to question, doubt, and ponder if it really happened. My daughter told me later that morning that she came into the living room, and I didn't respond to her when she asked me what I was looking at. However, I heard myself say, "I'm looking at an angel." However, she said, "No, mom, you never said a word." She recalled that I was sitting there in a trance, staring out the window, completely still. Seeing this, she walked over to the window to see if she could see something, but she could not, so she left me there in my trance. I was glad to have her as a confirmation to me of what occurred.

I knew as I journeyed to Atlanta that day, the guardian one was with me. I exceedingly felt his presence every step of the way. Allow me to share the next extraordinary moment of how the angel assisted in my son's transition.

I had arrived safely in Atlanta and met Paul Brian at the hotel where he was staying. I felt the most abnormal distance between me and my son that has never existed in our relationship. On this particular day, there was a chasm between us that alarmed me! We were very close and have never had a strain in our relationship. After hugging him numerous times through this invisible wall that was between us, it was time for me to leave. My heart was very weighed down as I walked away, trying to make sense of this burdensome intuition that something bad was going to happen.

While walking to the car, it was as if someone came up to me on my left side and put their mouth directly to my left ear and softly whispered in a very calm, clear, and audible voice that said, "Take a picture in case this is the last time that you see him." Here I was again, now with the third audible voice in less than 24 hours. Now coupled with the angelic visitation, this situation was becoming very unusual. Although I did take the picture, I cannot say that I was able to fully wrap my mind around what was just said to me, so my obedience seemed to be on autopilot. Nonetheless, I knew then that the heavy foreboding that something bad was going to happen came into laser focus with the realization that it was involving my son. However, his death was never a possibility to my conscious mind. How could it? What parent could bear the mere thought of their child leaving this earth before them? Although this was what my son had hoped would happen, it was my worst nightmare.

These two episodes were pivotal moments in my son's transition process. I now understand that the detachment that I was feeling was equivalent to the withdrawal phase of a terminally ill patient during the death and dying process. However, he was not terminally ill, but spiritually, he was on the brink of leaving this world for the next and final destination. I understand it all rather clearly now. Let's establish some biblical support by examining the fire, God, and angels in the Bible.

Chapter 16

A Cloud by Day and a Fire by Night

"Look on every exit as being an entrance somewhere else"
~Tom Stoppard.

Going back to our foundation of the importance of rightly discerning supernatural encounters, let's dissect and establish two to three witnesses from God's word regarding the angelic visitation. I went to the scriptures to examine references of fire being used by God or related to God. The first account that immediately came to my mind was the ***Exodus 13*** narrative of the Lord appearing as a cloud during the day to lead the Hebrews in the way they were to go and a pillar of fire was present to give them light at night. ***"Adonai went before them in a pillar of cloud by day to lead the way and in a pillar of fire by night to give them light. So they could travel both day and night. The pillar of cloud by day and the pillar of fire by night never departed from the people" (Exodus 13:21-22).***

This was not symbolism but a real phenomenon that God used to house the Lord's presence so that the Hebrews could behold His presence in the earth with their own eyes and so they would know they were not alone on their journey to an unknown land. How awesome is our God! Ironically, it is fascinating that my description of the angel was a white misty opaque color that looked like a cloud, and it had a flame of fire emanating from its being. I felt a strong feeling of protection, and now I know that God was my cloud by day and fire by night through this unimaginable journey of losing my child. The account of Moses' burning bush experience is probably the most thought of passage. ***Exodus 3:2 NIV*** recalls, ***"There the angel of the LORD appeared to him in flames of fire from within a bush. Moses saw that though the bush was on fire it did not burn up."***

In examining this narrative, the angel of the Lord spoke through the form of a burning bush that was not consumed. The flame itself was a real manifestation of the angel of the Lord. The burning flame emanating from the being that I saw never set any of the trees or branches on fire in my backyard. This is profoundly noteworthy because if it had been a flame of fire with natural physical properties, it would have been nearly impossible not to catch fire to the surrounding trees. As a matter of fact, I recall that when I initially saw the flame rapidly moving back and forth in the wooded yard, my biggest concern was a tree catching on fire. Well, it seemed that the flame moving back and forth was merely to get my attention because once I saw the form of the being, the flame stayed stationary in one spot just as he did. ***Exodus 19:18 (NIV): "Mount Sinai was covered with smoke, because the LORD descended on it in fire. The smoke billowed up from it like smoke from a furnace, and the whole mountain trembled violently."***

Deuteronomy 5:24 (NIV): "And you said, 'The LORD our God has shown us his glory and his majesty, and we have heard his voice from the fire. Today we have seen that a person can live even if God speaks to them.'"

Hebrews 1:7: "And regarding the angels He says, 'He makes His angels winds, and His servants a flame of fire.'"

These scriptures set my soul aflame because His word has been established as a witness that God displays Himself in a manner like fire. God can use any source of matter or nature that He desires to house His presence in or through because He created it all. It all belongs to Him. He conjoined the earthly and spiritual so that "as it is on earth, it is in heaven."

Hollywood has done its due diligence in their creative liberties bringing these stories to life on our movie screens to give us a visual depiction. Nonetheless, it's not fiction or fairy tales, but it's God's Holy Writ that reveals so many answers through scripture to always help guide us into the rightful discernment of His truth. One thing is for sure: ***"He will command His angels concerning you in all your ways" (Psalms 91:11 NIV).*** We must take comfort in this question: ***"Are not all angels ministering spirits sent to serve those who will inherit salvation?" (Hebrews 1:14 NIV).*** My reply is a resounding, "Yes, they are!"

Chapter 17

Heavenly Gifts

"God never gives someone a gift they are not capable of receiving" ~ **Pope Francis**

After the devastating news that my son had passed away, like an old-fashioned tape recorder rewinding, I could see the heavenly angel that I had seen the night before, as well as hear the voice that told me to take a picture in case that was the last time I saw him and feel the ensuing detachment between my son and me.

All of this coursed through my entire being as I reflected on knowing that the Ministering or Messenger Spirit was right there with me. The tugging and agonizing questions that I had as to why this spiritual phenomenon happened to me had been answered, and it was my worst fear—losing a child. The pain was immensely unbearable. I didn't know how I was going to sleep that night after getting the news and having to break it to my daughters and the rest of the family. I felt I was captured in a nightmare or having an out of body experience and watching someone else's tragedy. But it was mine; it was ours.

I was acutely drained by that night but felt it was keenly impossible for me to get any rest. My anxiety was beyond any ability on my own to manage. My chest hurt, and it seemed there was a ton of pressure each time I inhaled and exhaled. My insides rattled as if I were housed in a steel cage. I closed my eyes and began to take slow deep breaths in and out to stop the heart palpitations. I couldn't even pray. I wasn't angry at God or anything in that manner. I just couldn't loosen the suffocating noose from around my throat.

I don't remember falling asleep, but I was either asleep having a lucid dream, or I was experiencing an open vision; I do not know. In lucid dreams, you experience the events with heightened faculties of your five senses: touch, taste, smell, sight, and hearing. But not just the physical senses are involved, but the emotions and intellect as well are heightened to what can be perceived as very real. I understand the words of Paul so clearly now. ***"I know a man in Christ who fourteen years ago was caught up to the third heaven. Whether it was in the body or out of the body I do not know—God knows" (2 Corinthians 12:2 NIV).***

I'm not really sure how much time had passed while lying there, but all of a sudden, I was seeing myself and my daughters in bed from an aerial view. I was up and looking down. I was confused by this. Then suddenly, without any movement, I found myself in a very real place of pure impeccable bright whiteness. This white cannot be compared to any shade of white that I've ever seen on earth. Contained within the unblemished, spotless atmosphere was a living blanket of pure white clouds. The blanket of clouds appeared to be both a solid foundation but yet still light and weightless. I recently heard an account of a lady who had an experience of visiting heaven, and she described a cluster of angels that appeared like clouds. After recalling her testimony, I wondered if what I described as clouds were actually angels because they seemed to be alive with personality and an actual purpose.

As I was standing in pure bliss and tranquility, I began to hear the sweetest and most melodic and harmonious song that I've ever heard. Then there appeared a type of transportation mechanism but not like a car or truck. The closest thing to describe it would be a white, solid wood, fully enclosed baby crib with a solid headboard and footboard that resembled a vintage antique baby crib. It had a royal blue heart etched into the headboard. It is difficult to explain, but somehow, I perceived that this represented a baby boy. However, it was after the vision that I realized this was symbolic and not literal. The device was swaying back and forth in the blanket of clouds as if they had arms that were gently rocking it and passing it back and forth to the tempo of the music. The crib was swaying in a synchronized rhythm in perfect time with the soft melodic song that was being heralded in that vast domain. There was an exaltation of feelings of deep and endearing love. The "clouds" or angels tossed the transportation device through the atmosphere as if a thousand different mothers were taking turns passing an infant from one set of arms to another. What comfort. What peace.

Enraptured at this moment without time, the experience seemed to abruptly come to a screeching halt as the crib device had advanced beyond my frame of view. As if a curtain had been closed, I could no longer look through the window of eternity. I jumped and sat straight up in the bed with my heart racing 1000 beats per minute. I began asking my daughter Briana, "What was that song? Did you hear that song playing?" She expressed her confusion as she didn't hear a song. I know most gospel songs, but this was a completely new song that I had NEVER heard before and have not since then, although I've never stopped looking for it.

I immediately knew that this was another divine encounter. I deeply believe that I was in that area that I later read about in Mr. Sodi's account: ***"I looked abroad; we were just entering a region of*** *bright clouds, something like a glorious, glowing, earthly sunset, only far superior. The time had been very brief indeed, but we were actually slowing up in the great suburbs of the eternal kingdom."* (https://www.scribd.com/document/520527/Paradise-the-Holy-City-and-the-Glory-of-the-Throne-Elwood-Scott).

At that time, the Holy Spirit began to reveal the interpretation of what He was showing me through this encounter. First, I called my son, "Baby Boy." He was my only son, and this was a term of deep endearment. His contact name in my phone to this day is "Baby Boy." Immediately I understood God was communicating to me that He had my baby boy. But He also explained to me that although my son had been born-again, he had never matured or developed fully in the things of Christ, and as a babe in Christ, he had much to learn about His salvation. That song and vision should have soothed my spirit, but the pain was too fresh and intense at that moment. Nonetheless, as time would unfold, it did serve as a source of solace.

The next two days were filled with unbearable pain with the unimaginable daunting and emotionally draining task of planning my son's memorial service. The day was filled with gushing tears as visitors and calls began to come. I was terribly worried about my seven-month pregnant daughter. I had a deep concern for not wanting the severity of the emotions of shock and sorrow to cause her to go into preterm labor. After the funeral arrangements were made, I just had to get away, so I decided to travel back home to Alabama for a few days before the funeral. I couldn't explain why I needed to do this, but perhaps it was for my one daughter, who was also pregnant, in Alabama by herself with her two small children and husband. I felt I needed to get to them as well.

After arriving home, I was numb and in disbelief. Was this

really happening? I was crushed to the core. There was nothing left inside of me. I just had a piece of my soul die and was not sure that it would ever be resurrected. My son was gone.

But yet, I had this peace, and I wasn't sure if it was because of the previous visions that I just referenced. However, there was undoubtedly peace in my spirit but conflict in my mind. God hears and knows every thought before we ever think it. He heard me in distress, and He profoundly came to answer me, just as King David prayed numerous times.

I walked into my closet in a daze but intending to find the dress that I had envisioned wearing. I had a brand-new pair of shoes that I had never worn that I had just bought about two weeks before this tragedy. They were very glittery with shimmers of gold and silver. I thought how fitting to wear a black dress and have these dazzling shoes that gave me the sentiment of Dorothy in the Wizard of Oz; "There's no place like home." After all, I was preparing for the homegoing of my son. With that thought, I abruptly dropped to my knees from the weight of incomprehensible pain and emotions as the tears surged down my face.

The heat from my skin and salt from my tears mixed together to form a physical irritant that mimicked the inner irritant of my intense grief.

Within a blink of an eye or if someone had snapped their fingers, I was immediately immersed into a full open spiritual dimension in a vision. I was given the ability to see clearly as a first-person bystander in this spiritual place, and once again, I heard the words of Paul echoing in my spirit.

"I will go on to visions and revelations from the Lord. I know a man in Christ who fourteen years ago was caught up to the third heaven. Whether it was in the body or out of the

body I do not know—God knows. And I know that this man— whether in the body or apart from the body I do not know, but God knows— was caught up to paradise and heard inexpressible things." (2 Corinthians 12:1-5).

Whether in the body or out, I do not know. But what I do know is that the invisible veil was ripped, and I was granted access to witness the very transitioning of my son from this earthly life to the other side.

I beheld my son standing with his back to me in front of a broad-shouldered, muscular man sitting down on what appeared to be an old medieval-century wooden stool. His hands were folded in his lap and clasped together. He was postured as if he was a tribal elder prepared to hear a case. I knew that this man was a great man of authority. But there was an immense softness and love in his demeanor that seemed unfitting knowing how much authority he possessed. He had these deep, warm, brown eyes that were like an unlimited deep pool filled with love, and that love poured out and saturated that whole atmosphere. It was this enormity of love that made me weep. I was captivated by it. Oh, even now, my heart wails up inside of me from the impact of experiencing that love.

He was dressed in an ancient burnt orange tunic with a dark brown rope belt and leather sandals, much like the clothing worn in biblical movies. He had dark-chestnut-brown, thick, wavy hair that fell just shy of his shoulders, chiseled facial features outlined by a goatee with tanned skin.

He seemed so familiar. I knew that he was a holy man and not an angel. Although I felt that there were angels present, I did not see them. While standing in front of this holy one and taking in this atmosphere, my son exclaimed, "My mom was right! My mom was right!" and this immediately ensnared me. In a split second, I knew that he was recounting our conversations about what happens when we die and other spiritual things we had talked about just only two short months before he left the earth. I smiled at this and was astonished that the conversation was ordained by the Lord and not a mere coincidence. So many times, we have no idea why something happened or occurred the way it did. This is an aspect of those divine transitions that we previously discussed.

I was aware that I could see this first dimension of Earth at the same time I was there in that place. Allow me to explain. I saw my son's body lying on his back on the bathroom floor in his hotel room. Around a year after his death, I was able to confirm that my son was lying on the bathroom floor at some point after he was found struggling to breathe. However, I was not focused on this aspect of the vision at this time. I bore no interest in what was going on with his body, and soon I saw that neither was he. It is important to expound that as a mother, I should have become upset or distraught at seeing my son's body lying there dying. But I did not. It was as if that wasn't really him, not from a state of denial or anything like that, but it was impossible to associate that compromised human flesh as "my son" when I was standing right there watching him talk to this holy man! "Death" could not be perceived as death when you see the "dead" *living*! I did not carry one strand of grief at that moment. But let's continue on.

This Holy man beckoned my son to express his heart, his questions, and his anger. Without any reservations, my son freely began talking about such things as his anger with God over the sudden death of his girlfriend, things that he had questioned about religion, and the hurt of seeing Christians' harsh judgments and treatment of others and even him. Also, he asked why bad things happened to good people, and why was there so much suffering in the world? He even stated that it was hard for him to believe that God really loved him. But the most incredible spiritual exchange took place. There were immediate answers to and understanding of every question that he ever possessed. By the time he would utter the words, the answer or reassurance would instantly be given to him. I witnessed the fulfillment of the words from an old hymn that says, "We'll understand it better by and by." My son exclaimed with excitement, "Oh, I understand!" I get it now!" His previous questioning and reasoning about things of life seem to dissipate at a rapid pace in the presence of such love and acceptance that is beyond anything that you will ever know on this earth. All of the anger and confused thoughts about God and His love and goodness were healed in his soul.

But once that aspect had been completed, things began to take on a different form. I can only describe it in this manner. Once my son received healing in his soul, his spirit began to come under conviction about his actions and life on earth. My son judged his own actions and shortcomings based on what he now understood to be the truth about life and God. In one momentous moment, he understood everything about life, death, and everything in-between. My son had such joy to finally understand what he could not understand on this side of life. I was not privy to all of the innermost conversations between my son and the Holy man, but I knew it was a review to look at what he did with his life, choices he made, and his salvation when he accepted Christ as his Lord and Savior. I was able to understand that we judge ourselves in the light of this pure love, acceptance, and holiness of this place. I had longed to see this transformation in my son's life but never fully did on this side of the veil. But praise be to God, King of the Universe, I was given the spiritual eyes to see it come to pass in his life after life!

His soul had been healed. The soulish part of our triune-being encompasses the mind, will, and emotions. In life, our spirit man gets born-again by accepting Jesus Christ as the Son of God, the Messiah, who was crucified and resurrected on the third day and ascended to heaven. However, our soul still may suffer very deeply in our salvation walk. Furthermore, this broken soul can prevent or stunt spiritual growth. It's His desire and will is that we achieve soul healing in this life so that we can live life here more abundantly.

Although this man was postured like He was prepared to judge a matter, there was not harsh behavior as you would expect or think when envisioning judgment. Instead, He had only compassion, understanding, reconciliation, and forgiveness and granted a full pardon for my son amid my son's own self-condemnation. He was so focused and looked so lovingly and intently at my son as if he was the only person in the world that had ever existed. This was the LOVE that was overwhelming and hard to contain. The Holy Spirit gave me Jesus' words in *John 5:24-25*: *"Amen, amen I tell you, whoever hears My word and trusts the One who sent Me has eternal life. He does not come into judgment, but has passed over from death into life. Amen, amen I tell you, an hour is coming and is now here, when the dead will hear the voice of the Son of God. Those who hear will live!"* It makes me weep now even two years after the experience. This Holy and loving man assured him that he has always been with him and has never left him alone. He didn't condemn my son when He could have easily done so. Once again, the Holy Spirit took me to *John 3:17-18*: *"God did not send the Son into the world to condemn the world, but in order that the world might be saved through Him. The one who believes in Him is not condemned; but whoever does not believe has been condemned already because he has not put his trust in the one and only Son of God."* All of my life, I have been made to see God as this harsh and raging Higher Power that was ready to bring swift judgment and throw you into Hell for spitting on the sidewalk! (That's meant to draw a dramatic picture to the point that I'm making). Henceforth, I understand the true revelation of what it truly means for Jesus to be the Mediator who prays to the Father on our behalf, as noted in **Romans 8:34 (ESV): *"Who is to condemn? Christ Jesus is the one who died—more than that, who was raised is at the right hand of God, who indeed is interceding for us."***

But before I continue on, allow me to explain the poignant realization of how I came to understand the identity of the holy man and why I referenced him in that manner when I first started writing about this experience. It was only after I was "back to earth," if you will, and began to recount the experience and examine all that had transpired, did I understand who the holy man was. I reflected back on the whole vision with bewilderment and astonishment. I felt like I had been gone for ages. There was no sense of time—no today, yesterday, tomorrow or past, present, or future. It reminds me of what God meant when He exclaimed to Moses, "I AM that I AM!" The time just *was* that it *was*, no beginning or ending. It was as if what I was seeing had always been. It's extremely difficult to articulate.

The reminiscence of his attributes became so illuminating, as I could still feel the tangible presence of their effects on me and the atmospheric conditions around us. He was familiar to me as if I had known Him all of my life while I was "there." I never felt a question of who he was. However, while thinking with my fleshly mind, I initially thought that he was an ancient patriarch like Abraham or Moses. Moreover, as my reflection gave way to expounding on the magnitude of the love, grace, mercy, forgiveness, truth, justice, and redemption that exuded from his being, my spirit, like a wide-eyed child, bore full witness to the Spirit, that no mere earthen vessel of clay could possibly carry the purity and wholeness of the vastness of those characteristics. It is ONLY the Messiah who did and could do so. When He confirmed to my son that HE had always been with Him, I knew that to be true, both for him and even for myself. Not only was He YHWH, but He was also a best friend and brother. In the spirit, I knew this without one ounce of doubt, but once I was back in the flesh with its limited understanding, it was unbelievable to me that the person I saw was the Savior, Jesus Christ. I grappled with this as if I was Thomas, The Doubter, who was beholding the resurrected Yeshua but still had to put his finger inside of Christ's wounds. Consequently, with each episode of doubt, the Holy Spirit rushed in like the whirlwind that He is and reminded me again that the observed characteristics and attributes couldn't be fulfilled by a mere imperfect man like Abraham or Moses, but only the Spotless Lamb who was slain for the sins of the world, Yeshua HaMashiach (Hebrew for Jesus the Messiah).

But it was His eyes that I couldn't get out of my mind. It was as if I fell into their deep pools of love and was submerged by them. It was sometime later that I ran across an excerpt from Seneca Sodi's account of seeing Jesus in Heaven. I was able to finally see the words that could paint an adequate portrait of what I felt. Mr. Sodi describes the eyes of the God that sees all things. He sits high and looks low. Moses and Enoch recounted their presence there in the Celestial Kingdom for thousands of earthly years and have only just a taste of knowing the magnitude of God! The eyes that Mr. Sodi beheld was only a small ray of His light. The earth that is so large and grand in our eyes is just a footstool compared to the enormity of His being. We know the Lord tells Isaiah this when He said, *"Heaven is My throne and the earth is My footstool."* Our Supreme Father never gets weary, even though He knows all and sees all. He is always listening to lifted-up prayers. Psalm 121:2-4: *"I will lift up my eyes to the mountains-from where does my help come? My help comes from Adonai, Maker of heaven and earth. He will not let your foot slip. Your Keeper will not slumber. Behold, the Keeper of Israel neither slumbers nor sleeps."*

In the many days and months following my experience, although I am not an artist, I would find myself drawing pictures of His face and the complete scenery of the vision but, most of all, Him. I couldn't get any of it out of my mind. It was four years ago at the time of this writing, and I can remember it just as crystal clear as if it just happened. I fully understand what Jesus was referring to in *Matthew 18:3*: *"Amen, I tell you, unless you turn and become like children, you shall never enter the kingdom of heaven."* How difficult it is to find the words to put on paper because it pales and falls short of the emotions that I desire to convey to you right now! This was precisely how I felt while there in that place—like a child. Being like a child is different from being childish or immature. Receiving spiritual things like a child means to embrace it without reservations and doubt. It's embracing the innocence of unadulterated joy, peace, and thanksgiving for what Jesus has accomplished for you. Now I understand what Jesus was saying. Our adult intellect challenges and refutes everything. But a child takes it all at face value by pure faith. This was the reason why on earth, Jesus strongly cautioned anyone who came against a child's faith with these words in *Matthew 18:6 (CJB)*: *"And whoever ensnares one of these little ones who trust me, it would be better for him to have a millstone hung around his neck and be drowned in the open sea!"*

Another great perplexity of being in that spiritual domain versus the earth's was that my affection for my beloved son was that of a dear brother, instead of a mother to her son. Jesus was both of ours' chief Brother and Friend. It's only after I returned from the vision did I feel the human emotions and thoughts of him being my son. That's so incredible to me!

When you experience something supernatural by the spirit, it generates a different response from how you relate to it in the flesh. In the spirit, things that you see and feel are normal and natural as if this is how life has always been. I was void of any dismissive negative human emotions or skepticism. I had absolutely no sadness or pain for my son. But this was only because I was in the spirit. It was impossible to have any emotions other than love, joy, peace, adoration, thanksgiving. How marvelous is that? It's not until afterward when I began to write my story, did I feel the painful human emotions that flooded every fiber of my mind, body, and soul. But then this peace, joy, and thanksgiving would surface from the recesses of my spirit.

My son accepted the truth of His words and connected with Him as the Source of all that is, has been, and will be forevermore. Hallelujah! While my son's friends, strangers, and medical personnel were looking on his body struggling to "live," he was having the grandest and most phenomenal one-on-one conversation of his entire existence with the Master.

My son's rejuvenated spirit and exuberant joy were radiating from his being. He was smiling brightly like he was the noonday sun herself. Although I was enthralled by all of this, my attention was quickly refocused as I immediately sensed the arrival of someone's presence on my left side but not positioned directly beside me. I could see them distinctly in the distance, yet they were close at the same time. However, my son simultaneously also turned to his left as Christ was letting Him know that someone was there to see him.

Immediately upon looking to our left, three men were standing on a green grassy ridge. In the background to the right was a picturesque, brilliant, illustrious city that glistened like it was made with diamonds. As soon as Christ gave instructions to approach, they traveled at the speed of thought and appeared right in front of Him and my son. Let me add that no one spoke with their mouth. It was all through thought or mental telepathy. Now that I have studied some other experiencers, there's a commonality of description that communication was telepathic in the spiritual dimension. But you could see every single emotion and thought reflected on their faces. As I observed the men, I became keenly aware that I indeed knew them. They were dressed in pure white linen tunics and pants. This initially had bothered me when I was first journaling the experience because, in my mind, I thought that the only kind of heavenly garments were robes. I was relieved to discover several different accounts of experiencers that were taken to Heaven, explaining that there were different styles of dress in heaven based on one's preferences, just as we have different styles on earth. One experiencer stated that she knew a lady that must have lived during the antebellum era because she had on a dress from that period. It's really mind-boggling that life in Heaven resembles life on earth except without the bad and dead things of the earth. I have learned more and more what the scriptures mean by "Let it be done on earth as it is in Heaven." This actually means that Heaven is the real, and Earth is the model that's patterned after Heaven's likeness, just as we were created in God's likeness.

The first young man had a beaming smile on his face, and he

seemed to be the key greeter of the trio. In a matter of seconds, I quickly realized that it was my son's cousin, that we called Little Sonny, who had passed away many years ago at 26 years old, but it was as if they had just seen each other yesterday. Oh, how my heart starts leaping every time I recount this scene. Seneca Sodi spoke of how he recognized a woman in a group of joyous spirits when he was allowed to visit heaven for forty days: *"I cannot tell how we recognized each other but there is such a similarity of the spirit itself to the bodily features that we at once knew each other, and memory was so fresh that we seemed never to have forgotten anyone."*

He and my son embraced each other so tightly with such joy and affection. Oh, what a joyful reunion I beheld! I thought my son was going to burst at the seams. It was stupendous as I felt the same intense joy. I could feel its reverberation all through the atmosphere. A huge wide-eyed smile brightens my face and my heart as I intensely re-visualize that moment. The other two men I knew were older than Little Sonny, but that was not determined by their facial features. Little Sonny appeared to be around 25 or 27 years old. The two older gentlemen seemed to be about 30 years old. I knew that they had been older than Little Sonny in their earthly ages. In the spirit, there is a great perception of everything, and you are free of the limitations of the brain that we are yoked to with this body.

One of the men I was attentively focused on because I knew that I had known him in this life. My son had absolutely no tie to this earth, although he had me in his memory. I truly believe this was the primary reason that the Lord allowed me to hear him say, "My mother was right!" He did not want me to bear that sadness as the months and years would replay these scenes in my mind, thinking about the fact that he chose to stay. His flesh wanted nothing from this earth because of what he was given and seeing in his life after life—the real life!

I kept having that familiar older gentleman's face embedded in my mind and began to inquire of the Lord about who that was, especially as I started to write about this encounter and sought many fervent answers. I kept thinking about the man, and the Holy Spirit finally revealed to me that it was my mother's brother, Anthony, that we called Uncle. He had passed away approximately four or five years earlier. But I was in total stupefaction! "Surely that can't be him!" It was not my intention to dispute the Holy Spirit. But surely, I misheard what the Spirit was said, I thought.

When my uncle passed away, his face was worn and aged with bad dental health, and he was very thin. He was only 53 years old when he passed away from a heart attack, and life had not been the kindest to him. So, my intellect was getting the best of me. This flesh was contending with me, and it was winning. But I had no choice but to choose to believe that it was him. Therefore, the Spirit bore witness with my spirit that I saw my uncle and saw him in paradise; he was healthy, youthful, and without any imperfections. He was wearing white linen pants and a long tunic shirt. I just still couldn't believe it! But I realized that's why I felt especially close and familiar to him.

Amazingly, once again, the Holy Spirit set a time for me to experience something that would confirm that was indeed my uncle, just as He has every step of the way for every question or doubt through all of these encounters. A little over two years later, I was at my aunt Mary's house and looked at a picture on her coffee table, and my heart dropped to my feet. It was him! That was the man that I saw! It was a picture of my uncle in his twenties when he coached little league basketball. I had forgotten how he looked when he was younger. The feeling that came over me when looking at that picture can't be fully enunciated. I wanted to just shout to all of my family who was present and let them know that I saw uncle and he looked great, just like he did in this picture! Of course, I knew they may have met me with a police car and straight jacket a little later, so I had to just take a breath and exhale all of that enthusiasm and maintain my composure. My hands trembled as I snapped a picture of his picture with my phone. The third man was his Guardian Angel that has been assigned to him since birth, just as we all have at least one.

With the knowledge that it was my uncle, I understood the mature presence that he had versus Little Sonny's, who was more playful and jovial like the big cousin he is. On the other hand, my uncle was smiling but represented an authority figure, as he was my son's great uncle. They had been commissioned to take my son into Paradise. I wish that I could say that I was allowed to go into Paradise, but I was not. I was only permitted to know where they were going, and it was nearby. I did come to understand that Paradise is a part of Heaven like a suburb but not actually in the Heavenly City. I think of the thief on the cross that was told by Jesus, *"Today, you will be with me in Paradise."* However, while this was taking place, we were on the outside of Paradise and the Heavenly City. I can only describe it as a meeting station or holding place. But this is nothing like Catholicism's ideal of purgatory or any similar idea but more so a cleansing station. Thanks to the great testimony of Seneca Sodi, I can now confirm that there are portals on the outside of Heaven. *"I seemed now to be conscious that we were somewhere near one of the great entrances or gateways into the heavenly world, where all the souls from certain sections of the earth are brought and welcomed."* There have been several other accounts of testimonies in Heaven that spoke of the portals to Heaven.

They soon returned with my son, who was in utter awe and astonishment of what he had seen and experienced! Little Sonny was conveying a sentiment of "Man, you haven't seen nothing yet!" I could feel Sonny's longing for my son to stay. Then the Holy One let my son know that he had a choice. "You could go back into that body." He pointed with his hand in the direction of my son's body lying on the bathroom floor on the earth. I looked as well, and I saw him lying on his back on the bathroom floor of his hotel room. We could see in the earth's dimension while existing in the spiritual dimension as if they were together. Actually, they *were* existing simultaneously together, as I mentioned previously. This vision is what enabled me to understand this spiritual concept of the convergence of Heaven and earth.

My son looked at his body, but he clearly had no attachment to it whatsoever, and, to him, it appeared like some old dirty piece of clothing on the floor that he had no use for. He also began to reflect, and I heard his thoughts, similar to "Why would I want to go back to that thing and have to endure a life of struggle, heartache, and pain when I can stay here with all of this love, joy, and perfection? This is where I belong. I'm free!" He knew he was home.

The Lord knew what decision he would ultimately make. So, therefore, he knew it would be my son's appointed time. I have heard many accounts of NDEs that the majority of them were told that it was not their time, and also many others were given a choice. The ones who were told that it wasn't their time, were very upset to be informed of that and were even angry that they could not stay in this glorious place. **"But as it is written, Eye has not** *seen, nor ear heard, neither have entered into the heart of man, the things which God has prepared for them that love him"* (I Corinthians 2:9 AKJV).

Oh, what a glorious place that awaits us. My son beheld a glimpse of it, and it was magnificent. He had the joy that was set before him, just as Jesus did when He endured the cross. He saw us, and that gave Him endless and unwavering joy.

While I was in the spirit, I was so overjoyed for my son. I was feeling his spirit, and I celebrated with him to stay. It was so much love, joy, and peace in our heavenly home, and nothing about this earth made any sense, really. This was what life was really all about—coming back to live with Him forever. However, after this experience happened and my psyche was pulled back into my flesh, my mind and emotions boxed with me once again. I felt hurt that he didn't think about me, his sisters, or family, and how it would affect us if he stayed. The frailty of my human emotions was thinking, "How could he leave us like that?" Now I know that was completely ridiculous! There's no competition between the things of this life and the next in Christ.

In several NDE accounts, many expressed not having any concerns about this life, not that they didn't love their loved ones, but they were in such bliss, and it was impossible to want to leave it. One lady's account expressed how she felt such guilt because she was at peace with leaving her newborn baby and staying in heaven. She stated that she had a sense of peace that her baby daughter and husband would be alright, but she had to come back because it was not her time. But the Holy Spirit helped me to realize that my son chose life and to enter into Paradise escorted by precious loved ones, and he will be waiting for all of us. He didn't forget or have little regard for his family. But nothing of this earth can compare to where he was living now. Now it seems like an oxymoron to say that he chose life because that produces death on this earth. I watched my son leap for joy as he hugged his companions as they quickly headed back to Paradise, and he was out of my view.

Just as quickly as the portal into the spirit was opened, it was closed. I opened my eyes and was in a state of confusion for a moment because I was still in my closet and unsure of what had just happened or how long I had been there. Surely, I had been in the closet all night, but when I looked at the time, it had only been a few minutes, which seemed impossible to me. It seemed that I had witnessed an event that lasted a lifetime. With a smile, I remember that *"with the Lord one day is like a thousand years, and a thousand years is like one day."*

Chapter 18

The End of the Matter

"What a blessing that God allows a life to come through your body, and then allows you to place that body in a body bag and take it out. I had to say that there's a magnificent something that God has for me to do, to give me that level of completion. That level of experience. It's unspeakable" ~ Iyanla Vanzant

For anyone who has experienced a significant loss of a loved one, I know the pain, especially a child. Many have said that there is no greater pain than the loss of a child. I have the unfortunate experience of wholeheartedly bearing that truth. I was granted the privilege to see what we cannot see and to know what we did not know. I only saw a very small portion of the mystery of life, death, and everything in-between. There are thousands of modern-day miraculous experiences. We have avenues to spread these experiences to the masses to grant an insight into the most significant quandary of life, "What happens when we die?" Just as it takes faith to believe the words on the pages in the Bible, it takes faith to believe that He can use dreams, visions, and personal encounters to show us Himself. Ecclesiastes reminds us that there's nothing new under the sun. God is the same today as He was yesterday. He still longs to communicate with us.

I am so incredibly grateful to a loving Father who saw fit to show me the most awe-inspiring encounters and experiences that would prove to be comforting in the years to come after losing my precious dear son. I miss him every day. But four years later, when things get really hard, I draw on these moments that become more etched into my soul, unlike a mere memory or dream that fades away. This book is designed to keep this experience alive and breathing into the hearts and minds of all who read it and hear it. The main point of it all is, "Oh, how He loves you and me!"

If you've never accepted this loving Father God into your life through His Son Jesus Christ, then don't close these pages until you do. Life, death, and everything in-between can hinge on one split second from one moment to the next. Our eternity is built upon the foundation that we lay while residing here temporarily on earth. The Bible says in *I Corinthians 3:12 -15 (ESV), "Now if anyone builds on the foundation with gold, silver, precious stones, wood, hay, straw— each one's work will become manifest, for the Day will disclose it, because it will be revealed by fire, and the fire will test what sort of work each one has done. If the work that anyone has built on the foundation survives, he will receive a reward. If anyone's work is burned up, he will suffer loss, though he himself will be saved, but only as through fire."*

My conscience is clear, and God is my judge should I add to or take away anything that He instructed me to reveal. I release these words out of unadulterated obedience.

It is my prayer that you receive comfort in knowing that there is real life in the immeasurable heavenly realm after this life of flesh and bone has ended. Jesus promised us that He went to prepare a place for us and where He is, we will be with Him and live in mansions that He fashioned. I love the way *John 14:2 (NLV)* puts it: *"There is more than enough room in my Father's home. If this were not so, would I have told you that I am going to prepare a place for you? When everything is ready, I will come and get you, so that you will always be with Me where I am."*

Understand that when our loved ones go to Paradise, this is a temporary location for His people until the New Heaven and the New Earth, prophesied about in the Book of Revelation, comes down. *"Look! God's dwelling place is now among the people, and He will dwell with them. They will be His people, and God Himself will be with them and be their God. He will wipe every tear from their eyes. There will be no more death or mourning or crying or pain, for the old order of things has passed away"* (***Revelation 21:3-4***). We must encourage our hearts that the grave as we know it is not the end but only the beginning. I saw my son's life end at 27 years old but begin as a newborn babe in Christ to live and grow in the knowledge of Christ for all eternity. The words of Seneca Sodi sum up what I believe every transitioned loved one wants to tell us, if it were possible.

"I then said, 'If they could only know that you have brought us this news when they were lowering your cold body into the grave, if they could only see you here in all this glory, and us having this precious visit beneath there majestic trees of life, then they would lift their eyes on high and say: "Oh, that they had the wings of a dove, then would I fly away and be at rest" (Psalm 55:6).' Then with the anointed vision like the martyred Stephen of old, they might see heaven opened and the glories which the Son of God has prepared for all His children (Acts 7:56). If their eye of faith could only penetrate the veil that hides the future --if they only could, with spiritual vision, but behold these glories--if they could only hear even the echo of the melodies which we have just heard, and of which Paul

caught the tune of when transported to the third heaven, they would evermore say: 'For me to die is gain (Philippians 1:21).'"

IT IS FINISHED!

References

Scriptures quotations, unless otherwise marked, are from the Tree of Life (TLV) Translation of the Bible. Copyright © 2015 by The Messianic Jewish Family Bible Society.

Scriptures marked CJB are taken from the Complete Jewish Bible by David H. Stern. Copyright © 1998. All rights reserved. Used by permission of Messianic Jewish Publishers, 6120 Day Long Lane, Clarksville, MD 21029. www.messianicjewish.net.

Scripture quotations marked ESV are from the ESV® Bible (The Holy Bible, English Standard Version®), copyright © 2001 by Crossway, a publishing ministry of Good News Publishers. Used by permission. All rights reserved.

Scripture quotations marked NIV are from THE HOLY BIBLE, NEW INTERNATIONAL VERSION®, NIV® Copyright © 1973, 1978, 1984, 2011 by Biblica, Inc.® Used by permission. All rights reserved worldwide.

Scripture quotations marked NKJV are taken from the New King James Version®. Copyright © 1982 by Thomas Nelson. Used by permission. All rights reserved.

Scripture quotations marked WEB are taken from the World English Bible. Public domain. No Copyright.

Scripture quotations marked NASB taken from the New American Standard Bible® (NASB), Copyright © 1960, 1962, 1963, 1968, 1971, 1972, 1973, 1975, 1977, 1995 by The Lockman Foundation. Used by permission. www.Lockman.org.

Scripture quotations marked AMP taken from the Amplified® Bible (AMP), Copyright © 2015 by The Lockman Foundation. Used by permission. www.Lockman.org.

Scripture marked DARBY taken from The Holy Scriptures: A New Translation from the Original Languages by J. N. Darby. Public domain. No Copyright.

Scripture quotations marked NLT are taken from the Holy Bible, New Living Translation, copyright © 1996, 2004, 2015 by Tyndale House Foundation. Used by permission of Tyndale House Publishers, Inc., Carol Stream, Illinois 60188. All rights reserved.

Scripture quotations marked AKJV from The Authorized (King James) Version. Rights in the Authorized Version in the United Kingdom are vested in the Crown. Reproduced by permission of the Crown's patentee, Cambridge University Press.

Scripture quotations marked NLV are taken from the New Life Version, copyright © 1969 and 2003. Used by permission of Barbour Publishing, Inc., Uhrichsville, Ohio 44683. All rights reserved.

Scriptures marked BSB taken from The Holy Bible, Berean Study Bible, BSB, Copyright ©2016, 2018 by Bible Hub. Used by Permission. All Rights Reserved Worldwide.

Scriptures marked ABPE taken from The Original Aramaic New Testament in Plain English- with Psalms & Proverbs. Copyright © 2007; 8th edition Copyright © 2013. All rights reserved. Used by Permission.

Gospel of Nicodemus from the Biblical Apocrypha. Accessed on scriptural-truth.com.

Selections from the Book of Enoch accessed on scriptural-truth.com.

Selections from the Book of Jubilees accessed on scriptural-truth.com.

www.ingramcontent.com/pod-product-compliance
Lightning Source LLC
Chambersburg PA
CBHW031102080526
44587CB00011B/792